Dear Jim,

May God bless you beyond your imagination.

Robert L. Wallace

10/30/2011

This publication is designed to provide accurate and authoritative information in regard to the subject matter covered. It is sold with the understanding that the publisher is not engaged in rendering legal, accounting, or other professional service. If legal advice or other expert assistance is required, the services of a competent professional person should be sought.

Vice President and Publisher: Cynthia A. Zigmund
Acquisitions Editor: Jonathan Malysiak
Senior Managing Editor: Jack Kiburz
Interior Design: Lucy Jenkins
Cover Design: Design Solutions
Typesetting: Elizabeth Pitts

Published by Dearborn Trade Publishing
A Kaplan Professional Company

Printed in the United States of America

07   10 9 8 7 6 5 4 3 2

Library of Congress Cataloging-in-Publication Data

Wallace, Robert L., 1956–
    Strategic partnerships : an entrepreneur's guide to joint ventures and alliances / Robert L. Wallace.
        p.   cm.
    Includes index.
    ISBN 0-7931-8828-8 (6 × 9 hardcover)
    1. Joint ventures. 2. Strategic alliances (Business) 3. Entrepreneurship. 4. Joint ventures—Case studies. 5. Strategic alliances (Business)—Case studies. I. Title: Entrepreneur's guide to joint ventures and alliances.   II. Title.
    HD62.47.W338   2004
    658'.044–dc22

                                                                            2004012321

ACKNOWLEDGMENTS   v

ABOUT THE AUTHOR   vii

INTRODUCTION   ix

1. THE WHAT OF JOINT VENTURING   1

Case Study *Getting a New Perspective on the Challenge (The State of Maryland)*   16

2. THE WHY OF JOINT VENTURING   23

Case Study *Crossing the Aisle to Successful Joint Venturing (Michael Sales and Tim Allston)*   35

Case Study *Encouraging Supplier Alliances at Procter & Gamble*   41

3. THE STRATEGIC PARTNERSHIP MODEL *A Roadmap for a Successful Joint Venture*   47

Case Study *Building Suppliers While Building Autos at Ford Motor Company*   56

4. TRUST *It Must Be a Two-Way Street*   61

Case Study *Driving New Alliances at Microsoft*   75

5. DON'T LOSE YOUR MOGO   81

Case Study *Corporate Experience Helps Entrepreneurs Master the Alliance Equation (The Broadview Group Inc.)*   92

6. IS YOUR ORGANIZATION READY?   99

Case Study *Two Perspectives on Alliances from Freddie Mac*   114

7. KNOWING YOUR PARTNER   119

Case Study   *Observations on Alliance Success Factors from NMSDC's Leader*   133

8. MAKING IT WORK   139

Case Study   *Forging Early and Lasting Alliances at Toyota*   150

9. LEGAL ASPECTS AND EXIT STRATEGIES   155

Case Study   *Spreading the Strategic Alliance Message at Verizon*   165

10. WHEN LOSING IS WINNING   171

Case Study   *Eastman Kodak Company's Focus on Venture Relationships with Start-up Companies*   175

APPENDIX   *Sample Joint Venturing Related Business Agreements*   181

INDEX   201

The older I get the more humbled I become, as the years reveal ever so clearly the people that God has sent into my life to help me. Above all, I am grateful to God that He thought more of me than I did of myself. Never in my wildest imagination did I think that I would have accomplished so much in such a relatively short period of time. Thank you, Lord, for making this all possible.

I am especially indebted to my parents, Irene, Leon, Daniel, Hezekiah, and Edith, who sacrificed everything so that my wife and I could enjoy a better life than what they had. To my brothers, Richard, Ronald, Randy, and Raymond, thanks for encouraging me through our rough childhood and helping me to never give up on my dreams. My children, Robert Jr., Joshua, Ashana, Collin, Jordan, Taylor, James, Robert III, and Ayla, provide me motivation to dream, and I am grateful for that gift they have given me.

Besides my family, I believe that I have the greatest support team in the entire world. First is my smart and creative public relations manager, Michelle Rathman, CEO of Impact Communications, Inc. Michelle, along with her cohort, Lisa Landers, has been invaluable in helping me to bring my thoughts and ideas to life. Kudos to my "partner in crime," Jeanne Yocum, president of Tuscarora Communications, who has worked tirelessly with me on the writing of this book. She is a true professional and a pleasure to work with. Special thanks to my agent, Ms. Andrea Pedolsky, for finding new venues for my book ideas.

Working in conjunction with my external support team was my internal support team at my two companies—BiTHGroup

Technologies, Inc. and EntreTeach Learning Systems, LLC—who work diligently to keep the businesses running smoothly while I continuously dream up new ways to help businesses be successful. To Kim, Karen, Wayne, Donnell, Henry, Corey, and Ryan, I hope I have been a blessing to you, because you certainly have been a blessing to me.

None of my work would be possible were it not for the hundreds of entrepreneurs and corporations that have contributed to my research over the past 22 years. I am especially grateful to my friends at Toyota; Xerox; the Maryland State Governor's Office of Minority Affairs; Procter & Gamble; Allston Communications, Inc.; High Impact Marketing; Safeway; Verizon; The Broadview Group, Inc.; Bennett, Hutt & Company; AT&T; Cummins Inc.; Johnson Controls, Inc.; Ford Motor Company; Microsoft; NMSDC; Kodak; and Freddie Mac for providing valuable input into the research for this important book.

Finally, as my acknowledgments started with thanking God, I will end them by thanking my lifetime companion, friend, and love of my life—my lovely and adorable wife Carolyn. She is the epitome of the Proverbs 31 woman in all her splendor, magnificence, and virtuosity. Ever since our days as students at the University of Pennsylvania, the love of God and her love for me have been the only two things that I have been able to count on, no matter what. This world is a much better place because she is in it, and it gives me great honor to be able to call myself her husband.

Robert L. Wallace is an engineer, entrepreneur, author, speaker, educator, and consultant to microenterprises, small businesses, and corporations throughout the world. From his days as a graduate student at the Amos Tuck School of Business at Dartmouth College, he has studied the dynamics of business success and has become a recognized expert on entrepreneurship, intrapreneurship, joint venturing, and strategic partnering. Thousands of businesspeople have attended and benefited from the seminars and workshops that he offers nationally and internationally.

Wallace is the founder of three companies—BiTHGroup Technologies, Inc. (http://www.Bithgroup.com), EntreTeach Learning Systems, LLC (http://www.Entreteach.com), and Skelemetrics, LLC, a technology commercialization initiative. His 27 years of business and corporate experience at IBM, DuPont, Procter & Gamble, Westinghouse, and others included positions in general management, sales and marketing, engineering, research and development, business strategy, and operations management. He earned his Bachelor of Science degree in mechanical engineering and applied mechanics from the University of Pennsylvania's Towne School of Engineering and a Master of Business Administration from the Amos Tuck School of Business Administration at Dartmouth College, and he was awarded a Doctor of Humane Letters from Sojourner Douglas College.

Wallace is a published author many times over. His previous books include *Black Wealth through Black Entrepreneurship; Black Wealth: Your Road to Small Business Success; Soul Food: 52 Princi-*

ples for Black Entrepreneurial Success; and *The Ssese Principles: Guidelines for Creating Wealth through Faith.* He serves on numerous boards, including the GE Center for Financial Learning, Baltimore Workforce Investment Board, The Gilman School, Center Stage Playhouse, Maryland Hawk Corporation, State of Maryland Information Technology Board, and the Advanced Technology Commission of Maryland. He attends the Emmanuel Brinklow Seventh Day Adventist Church, is married to the former Carolyn Green, and lives in Howard County, Maryland, with his wife, six children, and two grandchildren.

For many years now, I've worked to identify the factors that contribute to entrepreneurial success. Having studied numerous businesses—both large and small—over the last two decades, one of the strategies I have consistently found to be among the most powerful for putting an entrepreneurial company on the path toward economic well-being is the use of joint ventures and strategic partnerships.

Done well, joint ventures provide both participating businesses with a chance to learn and benefit from each other, and to achieve results neither could achieve alone. In this book, you will learn just that—how to enter into joint ventures well so that your company can prosper in ways it never could by going it alone.

I first came to understand the unique power of joint ventures when I started studying the nature of entrepreneurship as a graduate student at the Amos Tuck School of Business at Dartmouth College in 1982. There I began a 20-year research project out of which I developed the Wallace 4 Quadrant Model of Entrepreneurial Success. This model, which I discussed at length in my first book, states that entrepreneurs must focus on four critical areas each day to increase their probability for long-term entrepreneurial success. These quadrants are:

1. Know yourself (maximize your ability and capacity to do work and to perform tasks).
2. Know your plan (develop a bridge to close the gap between the present and some future entrepreneurial event).

3. Know your universe (maintain harmony between your business strategy and the constraints and guidelines of the universe).
4. Know your resources and make them your own (leverage the success and failures of those who have gone before you).

Joint venturing has an extremely close connection with this model for entrepreneurial achievement. In fact, joint venturing is the logical next step for an entrepreneur to engage once he or she has gone through the analysis and internal critique that a serious navigation through my four-quadrant model demands. As I will discuss in this book, entering into a joint venture first requires analyzing your own organization (Quadrant 1). Planning (Quadrant 2) is also essential to joint venturing, as is knowing the environments in which you and your potential partner are working (Quadrant 3). Finally, you can significantly increase your odds of winning with a joint venture by studying how others have succeeded at making their partnerships work (Quadrant 4).

In the decade plus since I completed my formal study of entrepreneurship, I have had the opportunity to travel the country and even the world to meet with dozens of small business owners. In my education and training company, EntreTeach Learning Systems, LLC, we have actually segmented these business owners into three strategic categories—emerging entrepreneurs, embryonic entrepreneurs, and established entrepreneurs. Since 1994, I have provided workshops on joint venturing for these three groups of business people and have advised and consulted with numerous business owners and business support organizations. Everything I have learned from entrepreneurs during the course of my travels and from the participants in my presentations has strengthened my belief in the potency of joint ventures as a fuel for business growth and success.

THE ENVIRONMENT IS READY

Factors now at play in our economy make it both more feasible and more critical than ever for small business owners to leverage the power of joint venturing. These factors include:

Customer economy emerges. Dramatic shifts in how we conduct business are being forced by the fact that in the emerging Customer Economy, the customer is smart, well read, extremely demanding—often unforgiving—and frequently has numerous vendors from which to choose. This empowered customer is able to, and will force businesses to be able to, deliver at a much higher level with long-term consistency and sustainability. In my view, most businesses, on their own, will be unable to consistently meet the customer's expectations without committing major resources (financial and otherwise) over long periods of time. Of course, the alternative to going it alone in this new and uncharted economic terrain is to share the risk with other business entities that embrace a shared vision and parallel objectives.

Time and space are neutralized by technology. Advanced technology has significantly reduced the effect of time and space in the business world, which makes it possible for small and medium-sized businesses to successfully meet the needs of major corporations in ways they never could before. No longer do corporations and government entities automatically choose IBM over a much smaller firm, like my company, BiTHGroup Technologies Inc., just because IBM is bigger and has more resources. Larger companies have now seen or directly experienced enough examples of the far superior price-benefit ratios of smaller organizations that they, in many cases, are ready to embrace the notion of partnering with smaller businesses. This opens up a wide range of opportunities for small and medium-sized businesses to provide critical services to corporations in relationships that are more like partnerships than simply the buyer-seller relationships of the past.

Shifting demographics force change. In addition to price and quality benefits, another factor forcing both for-profit and governmental organizations to explore working relationships with non-traditional business entities is the dramatic shift in demographics in America and, for that matter, the world. According to the 2000 Census Report, African-Americans, Latinos, Asian-Americans, and Native Americans now make up more than one-third of the American population. This large ethnic population has more economic clout than ever before. According to the Selig Center for Economic Growth at the University of Georgia, the buying power of Hispanics will reach over $1 trillion by 2008. This is up an incredible 357 percent from what it was in 1990. Also by 2008, the combined buying power of African-Americans, Asian-Americans, and Native Americans will exceed $1.5 trillion, a 231 percent gain (from Jeffrey M. Humphreys, "The Multicultural Economy 2003: America's Minority Buying Power," *Georgia Business and Economic Conditions* 63, no. 2 (Second Quarter 2003): 2–6).

On the world scene, the population growth rate of the developing world is dramatically outdistancing the population growth rate of the developed world. As a matter of fact, the developing world's population is actually shrinking for the first time in more than 600 years. These population shifts and dynamics are forcing businesses to reach out and build strategic partnerships with small, minority-, and women-owned businesses that not only can bring new skills and talent to the table, but which also can assist their corporate partners in rapidly penetrating new and emerging consumer markets.

Downsizing is creating more entrepreneurs. The continued downsizing of corporate America is creating a new wave of entrepreneurs. I call this emerging economy, which will take place alongside the Customer Economy, the "Natural Entrepreneurial Economy." In this Natural Entrepreneurial Economy, more and more people will choose the entrepreneurial option because they will have no choice.

Downsizing will continue because the productivity gains that have been promised for the last 25 years are actually beginning to take hold in the back offices of corporate America. As a result, businesses are starting to live up to the "do more with less" doctrine. As productivity expands exponentially, businesses will require fewer and fewer workers, especially middle managers. (For the sake of discussion, let's assume that middle managers range in age from 35–60, earn $70,000 to $150,000 per year, and have jobs that involve managing people who do the actual work.) We will find more and more of these individuals, many of whom are well educated and highly trained in their fields, in the unemployment lines. As such people are repeatedly forced out of corporate jobs, many will determine that taking their economic fate into their own hands is the best choice for the long run. Bringing with them their corporate experience, many members of this new wave of entrepreneurs will be natural candidates for joint ventures. In fact, in many cases, these newly minted entrepreneurs will form joint ventures with previous corporate employers who can no longer afford to have them on the payroll but who still need their skills.

My hypothesis is that as the ranks of these natural entrepreneurs swell, the ones that are going to thrive are the ones who learn how to excel at joint ventures and partnerships. It is for this reason I have written a book that combines everything I have learned about joint venturing in the last two decades from my formal research with my hundreds of interactions with entrepreneurial businesses and corporations that are succeeding at joint venturing.

BEEN DOWN THIS PATH

If in the course of reading this book you are tempted to think that undertaking a joint venture is too complicated, too risky, or just plain too tough, please remember that I am not asking you to travel a path that I have not successfully traveled myself. In fact, from my earliest days as an entrepreneur, I have been involved in numerous joint ventures that have contributed to the success of my own business in many, many ways.

Like many of you who are reading this book right now, I was taught as a child and firmly believed that America is a true meritocracy. My father, who was a laborer, and my mother, who was a school teacher, taught my brothers and me that, if we went to good schools, got great educations, remained honest, and provided the best product and service, society would automatically recognize our value and contribution and promptly reward us. Consequently, I launched my business with the firm belief that my work would speak for itself and that I could achieve success all by my lonesome self. I became what I termed in my first book a "Blood and Guts Entrepreneur." So I blindly began my crooked journey to entrepreneurial success. Or so I thought.

It didn't take long for me to realize that, although I was a highly educated, intelligent, diligent, thorough, and trustworthy entrepreneur, I was also becoming a frustrated, bitter, angry, and, by the way, poor entrepreneur. As my world began crashing down around me, and as I saw other entrepreneurs who had a fraction of my talent excelling, I soon realized that what was missing from my business strategy were critical alliances and strategic partnerships that would help leverage my strengths and minimize my weaknesses. With this new strategic alliance game plan at the forefront, I soon began aggressively forging joint ventures and strategic alliances with hardware manufacturers, software developers, and service providers. In cases where it was determined that my company was too small to win multimillion-dollar contracts on its own, we brought in large companies to team with us so we could show the width, breadth, and depth to intimidate the competition and soothe the jittery nerves of the customer. This strategy began to work so well that instead of our company pushing itself onto other companies, those companies began to pull us into their deals because we were building a reputation as a "value-adding" teammate.

The experiences shared in this book are not meant to imply that joint venturing is simple or easy, and indeed, it can often be quite challenging. However, I can assure you that the rewards more than outweigh the difficulties. What I have attempted to do in this book is to provide you with the knowledge and tools you need to be a good joint venture partner. Armed with this information, you will be able to develop business relationships that will stimulate the growth of your business and your partner's business, provide professional growth opportunities for your employees, expand the tax base for your community, and help make America even more prosperous and maintain its business and economic leadership.

I wish you success as you strive to build a business that helps you gain economic well-being and achieve your full potential as a creative, successful human being.

1

THE WHAT OF JOINT VENTURING

"Business once grew by one of two ways: grass roots up, or by acquisition. Today businesses grow through alliances–all kinds of dangerous alliance, joint ventures, and customer partnering, which by the way, very few people understand."
PETER F. DRUCKER, MANAGEMENT GURU

When I was a graduate business student at the Amos Tuck School of Business at Dartmouth College, one of my favorite professors always admonished us that "if your business isn't growing, then it's dying. It might be a slow, quiet death, but it is still dying." In fact, many businesses are dying, and those that survive struggle with the challenge of how to grow their enterprises in these difficult times. It seems that since September 11, 2001, a time that changed forever the business terrain in which we must operate, more and more businesses are struggling with how to remain relevant, as well as afloat.

The challenges of growth and success that entrepreneurs face today are unparalleled in American history and maybe even world history. For example, historically, businesses have always assumed that the population of the country would continue to increase over time. This assumption created an imperative to build business models that were scaleable enough to capture this expanding market opportunity. However, if current demographic shifts continue and the birth rate in America continues to decline, we will, for the first time in our history, find our population aging and actually shrinking. The only reason that it is not shrinking now is due to immigration rates. Immigrants tend to maintain the birthrate of their adopted country at least for the first generation.

The other challenge entrepreneurs face in attempting to grow their businesses is the fact that the markets they serve and the competition that they contend with are no longer just local. Today we operate within the world economy and a worldwide competitive environment. Technology makes it possible for any company in the world to compete with any other company in the world for any given market. In addition, the fact that large corporations are "right-sizing" and the number of corporate employees who are pursuing entrepreneurial endeavors is exploding, the competitive environment for small businesses will only become more cutthroat and crowded, resulting in more and more companies chasing fewer and fewer deals. Given the perplexing reality outlined above, what's your plan for growing your business? This is undoubtedly a topic you've considered for many an hour. Ultimately, though, the strategies available for building a larger, more powerful, and more profitable organization narrow down to these three options:

I. **Grow organically.** This strategy involves plowing all retained earnings back into your company to scale the operation and develop new markets. Capital for growth under this model can also come from outside sources (e.g., banks, venture capitalists, or private investors). Under this strategy, you use the direct resources of your company to scale operations, develop new products, explore and capture new markets, and lobby political institutions to obtain political favor. While this method allows you to maintain the greatest degree of control over your company's destiny, total self-reliance comes with a significant downside. Having to self-generate all the necessary financial resources to support expansion usually means that growth will be limited and occur at a much slower pace. Your ability to respond to new opportunities will be constrained, and given the speed of change in the Customer Economy, it will be very difficult for most firms to keep up.

2. Grow through acquisitions. Using internally generated capital as well as funds provided by outside investors to purchase existing businesses will increase your capacity to deliver more goods and services to your current market and may help you penetrate new and emerging markets. The growth-through-acquisition model can produce rapid growth, but the challenges of integrating two organizations—especially if the company cultures differ in any serious way—can be significant. In fact, studies have shown that many mergers and acquisitions fail to produce the desired financial outcomes. This is why the business news regularly contains stories of corporate giants divesting companies they bought only a few years ago.

This has been a problem especially in the technology sector. As new technologies emerge and smaller companies are started up to commercialize these new technologies, at some point these smaller companies become targets of the larger companies. Unfortunately, too many of these "shotgun marriages" end up in divorce court. One example of this phenomenon is AT&T. AT&T has often acquired or built new businesses around new technologies (e.g., AT&T Wireless) only to later jettison those businesses due to, among many other reasons, incompatibility and a not–so-well-thought-out business integration strategy. In addition to the incompatibility issue, the price of using other people's money to support acquisitions is that you're giving over some degree of control to your financiers. As your control becomes more and more diluted, your influence on day-to-day decisions will usually follow suit. Using other people's capital for acquisitions is not necessarily a bad idea, but it is something that needs to be carefully considered before going down this path.

3. Aggressively create and leverage joint ventures and strategic partnerships, and embrace "co-opetition." As you will learn in detail in this book, the benefits of joining with another organization to tackle a shared business goal are many. While not without risks, such partnerships can be the foundation for long-term business growth and success.

Co-opetition is a creative spin on joint venturing and business alliances put forth by Adam Brandenburger, of the Harvard Business School, and Barry Nalebuff, of the Yale School of Management. In their book, *Co-opetition,* Nalebuff and Brandenburger say co-opetition occurs when a business cooperates with its competitor for mutual gain. This model is very prevalent in the technology economy. IBM, AOL, Apple, and Microsoft have embraced co-opetition as a means of expanding into new markets and even solidifying markets where they already dominate. When people think of joint venturing and alliances, their paradigm forces them to only consider partners who are not head-to-head competitors. While this is understandable, it may not be smart, especially given the impact that deregulation, accelerating technologies, and the merging of technological opportunities is having on the world economy.

My hypothesis is that, given the risks, constraints, resource allocation, velocity of change, and global reality that define the Customer Economy, for businesses to survive, they must master the art of building joint ventures and strategic alliances. Failure to master this art will result in more businesses experiencing slow, debilitating deaths. Similar to a person dying from carbon monoxide poisoning, this type of death is quiet, often painless, and just slows down your system until you fall asleep—a deadly sleep.

As T. Williams, supplier diversity manager for Toyota Motor Manufacturing North American, told me, "Companies that are more efficient in providing high quality business services have a much better chance of survival. We all have a relentless pursuit of cost reduction; that is what is driving us now. We must focus on eliminating waste in both conventional and unconventional ways. We have to challenge the fundamentals of how we conduct our business. We have to evaluate what is value-added and what is not value-added in every part of the supply-chain process." It is that kind of thinking among the leaders of America's large corporations that is driving the opportunity for smaller companies to join together—either with a larger company or with one their own size—to take advantage of this desire for value-added vendors at all parts of the supply chain.

EXPLORING THIS FOREIGN TERRITORY

Joint venturing is a new concept for many small business owners. But the rationale for joint venturing has never been stronger, and the number of opportunities to create such partnerships has never been greater than they are now. Thoroughly understanding the terrain of the joint venturing world, which may now be foreign territory to you, will help you avoid missteps and achieve success faster.

Joint venturing requires you to reach out into the business world and establish the kinds of close relationships where breaking bread together is a welcome activity. Sharing a meal with your potential joint venture partner in a relaxed atmosphere fosters the kind of candid business and personal discussion that lets you truly get to know each other. Getting to know each other on this level is essential, as I will discuss in Chapter 4. Then later in Chapter 8, I will discuss how to make sure your joint venture relationship remains vital and fun as it goes forward.

As you strive to achieve joint venturing success, you may find yourself facing obstacles. Some barriers may be within yourself and your organization. You may identify attitudes and behaviors that have to be put aside because they would stand in the way of your being a good partner.

For example, if we start with you, the CEO, your attitude and perspective on your business may have to change. The reason you are in business will be a major factor in determining what your propensity for joint venturing is. If you are in business because you want to create a job for yourself and maybe a few other people, then your business paradigm might not be well suited for a joint venturing opportunity. On the other hand, if your business paradigm is that you want to grow rapidly and build significant wealth in the process, you are probably an outstanding candidate for building joint ventures and strategic alliances.

Although joint venturing of some form is extremely common, not every business is adept at partnering, so you may run up against barriers in the organizations with whom you're attempting to partner. Also, in the new Customer Economy, one of the emerging barriers to building alliances is cultural misunderstanding. It is becoming more and more likely that your prospective alliance partner will be someone who does not look like you, who is not of the same gender, and who may not even speak your language. If you are a member of a minority group or a woman, these barriers may even include cultural attitudes that cause non-minority and non-female business owners to stereotype you and your business. In Chapter 4, I will address this topic in more depth.

It is imperative that you recognize potential barriers as early as possible in the process. Some of these external barriers may be easily addressed through communications and some analysis. Other barriers may be insurmountable, or the benefit of doing the deal may not justify the investment that it would take on your part to remove the barrier.

Keep in mind also the importance of taking action on these joint venture opportunities. Contrary to the popular belief that businesspeople are successful because they have mastered the art of making slow, careful, and deliberate decisions, most successful businesspeople also recognize that at some point you must "pull the trigger." Quick action is also an important key to finding and taking advantage of valuable joint venturing opportunities. Quick, decisive action is often a precursor to success in this area for these reasons:

Timing is everything in business. What makes sense today may not make sense next week. The burning need that a customer has today may be totally forgotten about next month. It is a bigger risk to delay doing a good joint venture today than hoping that the perfect one will come through tomorrow. Also, while you're taking the slow route to decision making, you may be missing out on other opportunities because you're stuck in idle, unable to make a decision on the opportunity in front of you right now.

There are no absolutely right or absolutely wrong answers. The CEO of a company often is a pioneer in developing new and novel ways to cut deals and to grow his or her business. There is no CEO handbook (at least not yet) and no holy grail that is guaranteed to lead to a successful venture. Often, after you've exhausted all your due diligence, it then becomes necessary to listen to your gut (aka your instinct) and go with that.

Fail fast. Success is really a numbers game. The more you play and engage the more you will win. If you don't swing at the ball, you will never hit a home run. If you don't jump in the pool, you will never learn to swim. Failing is a part of life and certainly is a part of business. Accept that reality and learn to fail fast. Failing fast suggests that you accelerate the process of discovery to quickly determine if the path you've chosen is indeed the correct one. If it turns out that it is, then God bless you. If not, then cut your losses quickly and move on to the next opportunity.

DEFINING A JOINT VENTURE

When I hold a workshop on joint venturing, I always start out by getting the audience to agree on a definition of the term so we're all clear on exactly what we're talking about. Here's the definition I present:

A joint venture is the coming together of two (or more) independent businesses for the sole purpose of achieving a specific outcome that would not have been achievable by any one of the firms alone.

If you break that description down, here are the elements that are present in order for a joint venture to exist:

First, a joint venture includes multiple independent companies. Most often, two businesses are involved, but there are instances in which more than two firms link together. Having more than two companies involved is becoming more and more common. Of course, there are particular industries, such as real estate, that lend themselves to a joint venturing business model. In this industry, projects typically are so large they require multiple players.

The word *independent* in the definition should not be overlooked. The challenges of bringing two totally separate organizations together for a joint venture are considerably different—and usually more complex—than when several divisions of one organization decide to take on a project together. Differences in company values and cultures, business goals, management structures, and many other factors have to be bridged when truly independent companies are involved. It is critical to be aware of this from the very start of discussions about the potential joint venture and all the way through to the ultimate completion of the joint venture's goal.

A joint venture has a clearly defined business purpose. I'll talk much more about why this is essential and how to establish the business purpose later, but in essence, a mission for the joint venture needs to be agreed upon up front. Also, this mission must benefit both organizations. A lopsided mission that allows one partner to reap a disproportionate share of the rewards will not lead to success; the major outcome of such a mission will be feelings of resentment and disappointment by the partner that is getting the short end of the stick. Understandably, these types of arrangements tend to be very short-lived.

The mission could not be achieved by either party without the aid of the other. If a company can achieve the mission by itself, little motivation exists for undertaking a joint venture, since such partnerships are not without their own challenges and risks. The interdependence that exists when neither side can achieve the mission alone is what holds the joint venture together and motivates the partnering companies to get over the hurdles that are sure to appear along the way.

Implicit in the requirement for a clearly defined business purpose is the need to agree on the supporting elements of the business purpose. These include the target customer base, the type of product or service to be sold, the support services to be provided, the vendors to be used, and the prices to be charged for goods and services. In addition, the partners must agree on the specific duties that each will undertake in support of the mission. Deciding who is going to do what—in great detail—before things get rolling avoids finger pointing and disappointment down the road.

THE JOINT VENTURE CONTINUUM

Now that we have looked at the characteristics of joint ventures, it's important to realize that this business relationship can take a variety of forms. Figure 1.1 is a scale I've developed to illustrate the range of formats that joint ventures can assume.

As you can see, a joint venture can vary in terms of the closeness or cohesiveness of the relationship that is formed between the two organizations. As you read the descriptions below, begin to think about which type of joint venture might be most attractive to you and your organization at this point in time. In other words, what type of partnering arrangement will make you most comfortable? Which one makes the most sense for your current business goals? These are important questions to consider before starting discussions with potential partners.

FIGURE 1.1 *The Joint Venture Continuum*

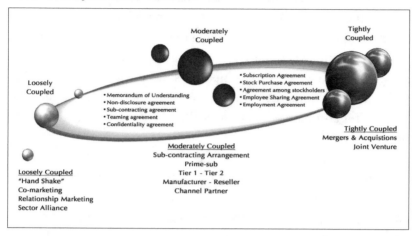

Here, then, are descriptions of the three points on the Joint Venture Continuum scale:

Loosely coupled joint ventures. Two companies in similar industries pool resources to go after larger contracts or enter new markets together. For instance, companies often reach out to other organizations to form a loosely coupled partnership in order to meet the specifications of a government contract.

A mutual service consortia, in which consulting firms with various specialties work together on client projects, is a good example of a loosely coupled joint venture. The firms might work together on only one client project for a short period of time while maintaining complete independence in their other business operations. But that one joint client may produce significant financial rewards or add luster to the firms' résumés that will attract more business in the future. Such a joint venture is a good way for a firm that has not worked in a particular industry but has easily transferable skills to get a foot in the door with companies in that industry. Such relationships are, of course, not limited to one-shot deals. Sometimes they last for years, with each partner calling in the other firm on an ad hoc basis. Oftentimes, firms that work together in this way do some marketing together, enabling both firms to present to the world what appears to be a larger entity with broader scope.

Even sole practitioners in some fields join together in loosely coupled joint ventures. This is particularly true in the marketing profession, where self-employed copywriters, art directors, publicists, Web site designers, and people in all sorts of marketing-related fields often form virtual partnerships that enable them to attract business from larger companies. With today's communications technology making such virtual partnerships appear seamless to clients, such arrangements are extremely common.

Another possible purpose for a loosely coupled joint venture might be to allow the partners to access advanced technology that is too expensive for either company to acquire alone. By initially sharing the cost of an expensive technology, each partner can use the technology to ramp up its business to a point where it can ultimately afford the technology on its own.

Moderately coupled joint ventures. Two independent companies move beyond an informal relationship to a more formal one. Typically, by this time, the two companies have become more familiar with one another and have had the opportunity to "try one another out." At this point, they like and trust one another enough to take the commitment one step further and two steps deeper. This is defined by a number of critical variables—time, depth, breadth, and willingness to open the organization to exposure.

For example, when two companies emerge into a moderately coupled joint venture they have spent a significant amount of time together and are willing to spend even more time together. While they certainly know more about one another than before the relationship started, they understand that more time together is needed. There is no substitute for spending quality time together. This time is not just spent in meetings and conferences but attending a ballgame together, going to dinner, introducing the spouses to one another, being in front of customers together, and wooing politicians and decision makers together.

Not only is spending time together critical, but "going deep" with one another is equally important. The old adage, "It's not what you know but who you know," is no longer valid in the Network-Centric Value Chain business environment. The new adage, "It's not only what you know and who you know but how well you know them!" reigns in the new competitive environment.

Going deep means focusing on making an investment in the relationship by taking ownership of better understanding your partner's true core competencies. How solid is their financial position? What is their real reputation within the vendor community, the industry, and among your customers? What about their infrastructure? Have your engineers had an opportunity to study their telecommunications infrastructure to assure that they are in fact able to handle the increased transactions that would come with an expanding customer base? Does your partner really have the political and business connections that he has been boasting about? The answers to these types of questions will lead you to a deeper understanding of your business partner.

Another requirement of a moderately coupled joint venture is to explore the options of breadth. Usually when two firms start down the path of engaging in some form of alliance, they focus on a narrow spectrum of opportunities. They might first start by introducing each other to each other's customers (assuming they are in non-competing industries). Or the two companies might begin by reselling each other's products. As the relationship successfully matures, the two firms will begin to expand the breadth of economic opportunities that they want to work on together.

The final way you know that you've moved to a moderately coupled joint venture is when both companies are more open and more willing to expose their weaknesses. No one likes to expose their weaknesses. To a degree all businesses harbor some form of inferiority complex. However, getting the most out of an alliance requires taking a risk with one another, understanding that you could get hurt in the process but believing that you won't.

Some moderately coupled partnerships take the form of prime-contractor/subcontractor relationships. Outsourcing arrangements in which a company agrees to have another company take over its information technology or marketing function, for instance, meet the definition of a moderately coupled joint venture.

Tightly coupled joint ventures. These extend the moderately coupled joint venture requirements, again defined by time committed to the venture, the depth of the relationship, the breadth of cooperative opportunities that the two firms commit to pursue collectively, and each firm's willingness to expose its weaknesses to the other partner. Tightly coupled joint ventures usually involve a formal integration of resources, infrastructure, processes, and services.

Commitments in these relationships tend to be high; the partners tend to develop joint activities in many functions, operations often overlap, and the relationship thus creates substantial change within each organization. When companies in different industries with different but complementary skills link their capabilities to create value for ultimate users, it usually requires a tightly coupled joint venture to make it work.

Another defining criterion for tightly coupled joint ventures is the amount of legal paperwork involved in consummating a deal of this nature. There is heavy reliance on the services of attorneys and accountants and a great amount of time is necessary to exercise proper due diligence. The legal issues of joint venturing will be discussed in Chapter 9.

The beauty of this Joint Venture Continuum is that you don't have to jump into joint venturing with both feet. You can choose to first dabble with a loosely coupled joint venture to see how you like working with another business to begin with and also to see if you specifically like any particular organization as a partner. If you find you are comfortable with a loosely coupled joint venture, then you might choose to move further to the right on the continuum and explore a moderately coupled partnering. Eventually, you might even want to form a tightly coupled joint venture.

If you decide your first joint venture was not a good experience, please don't give up on the whole concept. That particular partner may not have been right for you and your company. Don't hesitate to try another partner. Like anything worthwhile, joint venturing takes time and effort to master. And while we're not all born with the whole panoply of skills and attitudes needed to be good at joint venturing, I am firmly convinced these skills and attitudes can be mastered over time, which is what I intend to help you to do with this book.

Keep in mind also that the form of business alliance you engage in will probably vary over the life of the relationship and over the life of your company. If yours is a young company just starting out, you might begin with a number of loosely coupled alliance arrangements. This approach will give you enough time to understand your strengths and weaknesses better and become more comfortable with the "process" of identifying and building partnership arrangements. Loosely coupled alliances are low risk. If a company is unsure of itself or of its potential partner, a loose arrangement lets everyone in the relationship "try it out" to see if they like it and can live with it.

As your company begins to grow and establish a name for itself, you may want to migrate to business arrangements that are more moderately coupled. This approach does not suggest that you cannot continue with pursuing loosely coupled arrangements, but you will find that your return on investment in the relationship will tend to be greater when you are able to secure more moderately coupled arrangements.

Finally, after you have established the business, built market share, mind share, and brand share, you might want to consider taking the business to the next level by either merging your company with another company or by committing resources from your company into a new company into which your alliance partner also puts resources. This third, independent company would run like a stand-alone corporate entity, even though it is partially owned by both companies.

EXIT RAMP

One final aspect of the Joint Venture Continuum I want to point out to you before leaving this topic is that, as you move across the continuum from loosely to moderately to tightly coupled, your ability to walk away from the partnership without paying a heavy price decreases. I'm going to talk in depth about the importance of creating an exit strategy before signing onto a joint venture later, but for now, keep in mind that getting out gets progressively tougher the closer the relationship is.

In a loosely coupled relationship, the decision to halt joint activities is pretty simple. You wait until the current joint project is completed and then agree to go your separate ways. Complications can arise, revenues may take a short-term hit, and feelings may even be hurt, but generally speaking, dissolving the relationship is relatively simple.

Even with a moderately coupled joint venture, disengaging may not be too difficult, although more significant financial consequences may be entailed. If, for instance, your company serves as a subcontractor for a prime contractor that decides to let you go because it can get a better price elsewhere, this may be a painful financial experience. But your operations are not so intertwined that you couldn't go on operating on your own.

GETTING A NEW PERSPECTIVE ON THE CHALLENGE

As Special Secretary for the State of Maryland Governor's Office of Minority Affairs, Sharon R. Pinder heads an office that is in charge of advocating, promoting, and supporting the constituent base of minority- and women-owned businesses in Maryland. Although Maryland is a small state, it has 82,000 minority-owned firms and 112,000 women-owned firms. This gives Pinder a constituent base of nearly 200,000 businesses, which is 50 percent of all firms in the state. She is determined to make Maryland's Minority Business Enterprise Program a model for other states.

Sharon Pinder has over 20 years of experience successfully leading change for Fortune 500 corporations and as a minority business entrepreneur. As a result of her business success, she has received many honors, including being named the 2004 Distinguished Alumnae of the Year by the University of Maryland, the 2003 Award of Excellence from the Maryland Women for Responsive Government, the 2002 Outstanding Leader of the Year by Leadership Maryland, and one of Maryland's Top 100 Women for 2002.

In her current position, which she assumed in 2003, and in her private sector experience, Pinder has both witnessed and participated in many strategic partnerships. She shares what she's learned from both her private and public sector viewing posts here.

What do you see going on as far as joint venturing among your constituency?

Pinder: Over the past year in this job, I've been encouraged by the growing number of minority- and women-owned companies doing joint ventures or alliances. There have been some best practices that have heightened the awareness of this model. This strategy enables smaller companies to compete with larger firms, and it increases their pool of available opportunities.

Over the last year, I've witnessed some creative competitive strategies. The procurement model for the State of Maryland currently consists largely of bundled, multiyear, and competitive bid contracts. Given this environment, I'd like to share three examples of successful joint ventures.

One of the State's primary procurement agencies awarded a major information technology contract to a minority prime contractor with minority subcontractors. They won this competitive bid contract against some of the country's top industry information technology leaders because they had the right combination of skill, expertise, and business savvy. As standalone companies, they were successful in their own right. Any one of the companies could have been the prime contractor. They made a decision to partner and determined the right combination of leadership and teaming that resulted in the win.

Another agency put out a request for proposal (RFP) to provide specialized transportation services. This was a multi-million-dollar, multiyear contract that was about to expire. During the duration of the previous contract, there had been several minority subcontractors that participated on the contract. For the new RFP, these subcontractors decided to pool their collective experiences and resources in an attempt to win the contract as a prime. They felt the timing was right, and they had the customer relationship and multiyear experience in delivering the services on the contract. They also recognized their competitors in this bid were companies that were much larger and had more experience, and in some cases, their competitors held similar contracts in other states. They put together an excellent proposal. Unfortunately, they did not win the contract but only because the State reversed its decision to unbundle the contract. I am confident they will find other opportunities as a group.

One of the most fascinating ventures I've watched included a group of individuals that had built very successful businesses in different business acumens. Their acumens included real estate, health care, financial investment, and construction. Although they were successful in building their individual businesses, they decided to form an alliance for the purposes of leveraging resources to conquer a different business model. When we met, they were looking into a variety of business opportunities, including franchising and commercial real estate development. They represent a best practice of thinking outside the box and expanding their business horizons. These entrepreneurs understand the upside of joint ventures and have the wherewithal, creativity, and resources to pursue large complex deals.

Do you see facilitating alliances and joint ventures as being part of your strategy to help women and minority businesses in Maryland to scale quickly?

Pinder: Absolutely. I firmly believe that business is about turning good relationships into money. Our primary goal as a business-friendly state is to foster an environment that supports the growth of all businesses. Governor Robert L. Ehrlich and Lt. Governor Michael S. Steele understand the importance of providing the infrastructure and procurement opportunities. The State of Maryland spends billions of dollars in procuring goods and services. Our strategy is to devise solutions that will ensure the sustainability and survivability of minority- and women-owned businesses. In 2004, we saw an opportunity to level the playing field by designating, via legislation, a portion of those dollars (10 percent) exclusively for small businesses. Minority- and women-owned businesses are the direct beneficiaries of this landmark legislation, passed during the 2004 General Assembly session. This, coupled with the current 25 percent MBE goal, strategically creates a "sandbox" that enables minority- and women-owned businesses to compete in a more open environment. It opens the door for these businesses to engage in business practices as alliances and joint ventures in order to broaden their base of business.

Even with all of these reforms, Maryland still has one of the most complex procurement programs. The quickest way for firms to gain entry to state procurement opportunities remains to partner with firms that have already mastered the system. To further encourage partnering, the Governor has also created through Executive Order the state's first mentor protégée program.

To facilitate international partnerships, we use trade missions. Over the last year, the State of Maryland led two trade missions aimed at minority- and women-owned businesses. The purpose of the trade missions is to provide the opportunity for the state's women- and minority-owned businesses to do international trade. In 2003 and 2004, we completed a trade mission to Barbados and one to Africa. Again, this is another avenue to promote joint ventures, partnerships, and alliances, particularly on an international scale.

Are joint ventures and alliances necessary for survival among your constituency?

Pinder: Yes, definitely, because it is about growth. The economy certainly is the primary indicator of how much the State will spend in a given fiscal year. The economic indicators have resulted in less spending and have created a sense of urgency for minority- and women-owned businesses to look at alternative methods for deriving revenue. I often advise firms to really examine their market plans and to carefully make the assessment of what they can realistically obtain through public sector procurement opportunities. With this growing trend towards bundling in private and public sector organizations, it is impossible for firms to independently compete in a marketplace. With entrepreneurship on the rise, joint ventures and alliances become a great tool to deal with economies of scale for survival.

Have you seen differences in how well joint ventures work when a small business teams up with a very large business?

Pinder: There are several factors that I think greatly influence the trend of teaming large and small businesses. The growing swing in demographics—as the minority becomes the majority—was a rude awakening for large corporations doing business with organizations that suddenly enforced women and minority business goals. As accountability for participation of minority- and women-owned businesses increased, so did the notion that larger businesses had to begin to accommodate their smaller competitors. The other factor I believe heavily influenced this trend of teaming was the introduction of the Internet. The use of the Internet as a delivery vehicle levels the playing field for small businesses. A smaller company can eat the lunch of a larger company, because the smaller companies were more agile and cost effective and could deliver quality solutions faster. During my private sector experience as an entrepreneur, I remember being courted by large corporations, largely because they knew our services could complement their solutions. Additionally, what they valued were relationships we had already established with business entities they were pursuing. The fact that larger companies now see the value of partnership with smaller businesses is a paradigm shift in business focus. In the past, the best you could hope for was an appointment with the right person. At the end of the day, what was driving the change in behavior was that larger companies knew they were leaving money on the table.

My personal experience has been that larger companies didn't initially have a comfort level with letting a smaller business take the lead. They were used to being the 900-pound gorilla. The success of the relationship was mainly driven by customer satisfaction and, ultimately, by the players involved on both sides.

How was that relationship maintained during the course of the contract and beyond?

Pinder: Sometimes it was a real struggle. An old business adage sums up one of the biggest challenges: "He who has the gold rules." However, the key to teaming with a very large business is to ensure the ground rules are established up front. When all participants agree on who is driving the train, success is possible.

In business, we always talk about how success is driven by relationships. This isn't any different. If the relationship is established and includes mutual respect, then it works. If you are treated as an inferior partner because of your size, gender, or race, it won't work and the relationship is just more painful than it's worth.

Have you observed that big companies have a hard time allowing smaller companies to lead when it makes sense to do it that way?

Pinder: It depends. If the smaller company brings the larger company to the party, they have to dance to their tune. However, I have observed that it can be personality driven. If the team or participants from the big company have no experience in true partnership, then it is a problem. I remember working for a Fortune 500 company that showed a certain arrogance as the larger company. This arrogance can lead to exploitation instead of partnership. Always speak with existing partners to ensure you do not partner with a very large business that has a culture that makes partnering with a smaller business risky.

What attitudes do you see that keep minority business owners from doing joint ventures?

Pinder: Pride of ownership and loss of control are the key concerns among minority- and women-owned businesses. A great number of minority business owners are first-generation entrepreneurs and have sacrificed so much to get where they are in the business life cycle. Unfortunately, the "I must be in charge" attitude often prevents us from taking advantage of opportunities. Loss of control is a genuine concern when you do not have a level of trust with the corporate culture and individuals involved in the deal.

Do you find the pride-of-ownership obstacle to be more of an issue for minority businesses than for large mainstream businesses?

Pinder: Yes, most definitely. I think some business owners become too personally attached. Mainstream businesses cannot compare to entrepreneurs on this issue. One of the mistakes I made when I started out in the entrepreneur space was that I thought I had to do it all. I had "business trust" issues.

I have seen minority and women business owners lose valuable and dedicated employees, because they didn't understand the value of sharing the wealth with their team. It takes so many components to grow a successful business. You can't grow it on your own; so much is tied to your workforce. I think larger businesses better understand the value of their workforce and are willing to provide incentives.

Pride of ownership clouds business judgment, and I've seen deals blown because of this fear of lack of control. I believe that minority and women business owners are becoming more business mature. They understand it is a matter of survival. A lot of what slows us down in terms of joint venturing or other growth strategies is that we just don't have the experience yet. While the social/economic status of minority and women business owners has changed over the last 20 years or so, we're still pretty young in this entrepreneur thing. We've had great entrepreneurs in the past—my father was an entrepreneur—but most of us don't have the role models and mentors we need. What we have to do is seek out that angel who has had that experience. It gets back to surrounding yourself with people who can help you through the process.

How do small business owners find their angel?

Pinder: As an entrepreneur, I purposely sought out organizations that took me into arenas that were mainly outside my own network. I made myself available for boards and commissions and completed the Leadership Maryland program. Once I established those key relationships, I sought mentors who could help me with my business. I also established a "kitchen cabinet" of advisors. I have now taken that strategy and applied it in my public sector role as Special Secretary for the Governor's Office of Minority Affairs.

2

THE WHY OF JOINT VENTURING

"If you do not seek out helpers and allies,
then you will be isolated and weak."
SUN TZU, *THE ART OF WAR*

Now that we have looked at what a joint venture is and the forms it can take, the next issues that come to mind are usually the "why" questions: Why should you enter into a joint venture? Why should you try something you've never tried before and risk failure? Why should you take time from your core business to reach out to another organization that may not even be interested in partnering with you?

Many of the entrepreneurs who struggle with these questions conclude that they must either enter into joint ventures and partner or die. From my analysis, there are no other viable alternatives to long-term, sustainable growth. As entrepreneurs look to find creative and predictable ways to grow their businesses in the Customer Economy, many will conclude that they must become proficient at developing joint ventures because the business growth potential is tremendous. The incentives for entering into a joint venture are illustrated and summarized in Figure 2.1.

FIGURE 2.1 *The Joint Venture Incentive*

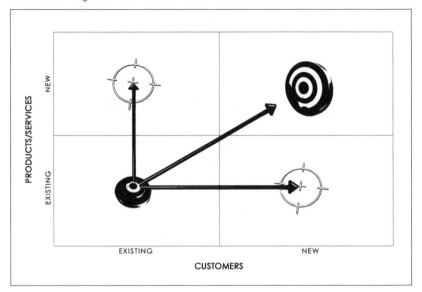

As the chart in Figure 2.1 shows, through a joint venture, your company can achieve growth by selling:

New products and services to existing customers. In this scenario, you link with a partner to provide their products or services to your current customers, or the two of you jointly develop new products for your existing customers.

Existing products and services to new customers. A partner is often able to quickly open up new markets to you that would take you some time to break into on your own. By forming an alliance with a company that is already active in a market that you've targeted, you can shorten your entry time into that arena. Instead of knocking on doors as a stranger, you have the benefit of having your partner open those doors for you.

New products and services to new customers. Together, you and your joint venture partner can combine your core capabilities to create something new and exciting that will attract new customers for both of you. Bringing two organizations together can create synergy that shortens both the new product development and sales cycles and puts you both on the fast track to market expansion. Also, by developing a new product or service with a partner, you spread the risk of failure over two organizations instead of putting it all onto your own company.

Obviously, you can also grow your company by selling more existing products and services to existing customers. But let's be realistic. If you're selling to other businesses—unless you're in an industry in which your customers are experiencing significant growth themselves—this type of growth is likely to be very gradual. So you need to be either in the position to offer these customers something new or to reach out to new clients with either existing or new offerings to support the significant annual growth you desire.

Likewise, if you're selling a consumer product or service, your ability to grow by significantly increasing the volume sold to existing customers generally is not huge. Here again, you need to constantly reach out for new customers or offer existing customers something new and innovative to achieve consistent growth.

ACCEPTING THE PARADIGM SHIFT

Some entrepreneurs are leery of joint venturing because their business philosophy stresses the importance of standing on their own two feet and doing things for themselves. If you started out with scarce resources and toiled on your own for many years to achieve success, it can be difficult to think of doing it any other way. Giving up even a little control may be hard to contemplate.

If you are a woman business owner or a minority business owner, you may have had little choice but to do everything yourself. In the past, lending programs geared toward your business-growth needs were scarce, so you had to bootstrap your organization, using personal funds and what you could borrow from relatives or friends. Beyond gaining access to capital sources, women

Where to Find Joint Venture Partners

Sometimes, if you're lucky, you may be on the receiving end of a call from an interested party who is seeking a joint venture partner. Perhaps a current client realizes the value you could bring to the table for a new project they're considering. Or a company that needs your capabilities to move a new project forward might hear good things about you from someone else. Getting such calls of interest is a gratifying experience since it confirms that your company's public image is a positive one.

While having the phone ring with a new opportunity is great, it's not something you can rely on to happen. And certainly the timing of such calls may not match your own business growth timetable. So, instead of waiting for opportunity to knock at your door, you have to go out and meet it halfway. Networking is the name of the game in joint venturing. You can't build alliances sitting in your office from 9 to 5 and then going home for the evening. You have to get out and mingle and constantly increase your circle of acquaintances.

When you're thinking of where you might meet potential alliance partners, don't limit yourself to business associations or industry organizations. Yes, you should be part of your local Chamber of Commerce or Rotary, but being active in civic affairs, volunteering to serve on nonprofit boards, or even participating in your children's school activities are fine ways to get to meet other business people who are similarly involved in the community.

Be as creative as you can. Just because business is not the main topic of an event doesn't mean it might not be fertile networking grounds if it gives you an opportunity to interact with new people. The only guideline is to constantly create the opportunity to meet new people, some of whom are bound to share overlapping common business interests with you.

If the word "networking" makes you groan, don't despair. Yes, some people are natural networkers, but most people need help learning how to put themselves out there and, fortunately, plenty of resources are available in the form of books and tapes to help you gain the confidence needed to mix and mingle.

Once you have a pool of alliance candidates, the next step is to determine which companies in that group are potentially good matches for the joint venture you're contemplating pursuing. This is the group that you'll want to get to know better through the due diligence process I'll talk about in Chapter 7. At the same time, however, stay in touch with the rest of your potential alliance pool because even though a company is not a good match for your current project, a year from now they might be just what you need.

and minority entrepreneurs also have had a difficult time gaining access to markets. Despite the technical, managerial, and leadership skills to add value to customers that these entrepreneurs bring to the table, some institutions still resist the participation of these new, intelligent, and energetic business leaders. While the resources available to women- and minority-owned businesses have improved, the situation is still not ideal, so the notion of having to do it all by yourself is still heavily ingrained in many business owners' minds.

To even consider undertaking a joint venture requires a shift in this paradigm. You must change how you think about your business and specifically how you believe you can best grow that business. Changing the paradigm requires accepting that going it *totally* alone in today's complex business world may simply no longer be possible for the vast majority of small businesses.

Always keep in mind that you don't have to bet your whole company's future on your very first alliance. You can start out small and build both your company's competence as a joint venture partner and your own confidence in the wisdom of joint venturing as a business growth mechanism. And while some joint venture partner relationships do eventually result in one organization subsuming the other, if that's not something you wish to have happen with your business, you can design your alliances to have different outcomes. (See Chapter 9 for a discussion of exit strategies.)

THE BUT SYNDROME

The doubts that enter your mind as you begin to consider a joint venture may cause a cacophony of noise that can make you want to forget the whole idea. This noise can get particularly loud when you begin to consider a specific partner. I call what happens next the "But Syndrome." You start to look at a possible partner and you immediately begin to come up with objections about why forming an alliance with that particular company won't work. You think, *Yes, they're a possibility* but *they're:*

- Too small
- Too large
- In the wrong geographic location
- Minority-owned
- Majority-owned
- Woman-owned

When this happens, you need to turn the But Syndrome on its head and use it to add value instead of to detract from the attractiveness of a partner. Thus, you think something like, *They're too small,* but *they bring:*

- Customer relationships
- A different way of thinking
- Access to domestically emerging markets (DEMs)
- Access to internationally emerging markets (IEMs)
- Technical competence
- Political relationships
- Geographical penetration
- Industry sector penetration
- Engineering niches
- Marketing savvy

The list of skills, know-how, and vital connections a potential partner can offer is endless. By carefully evaluating this list, you can effectively counter the But Syndrome.

THE CHESS FACTOR

In addition to understanding what a joint venture can do for your business, it is also helpful to look at the big picture issues that are driving the growth of joint venturing. I refer to these issues collectively as the "CHESS" factor, as in:

- **C**ompetition
- **H**istorical influences
- **E**conomic climate
- **S**ocietal events
- **S**trategic alliances = survival

Let's look at the influence each component of the CHESS factor is having on the growth of joint venturing:

Competition

Joint venturing is becoming the norm instead of the exception in business today. "Everybody" is doing it, which means your competitors are probably doing it. The question to consider is whether you can afford to be left behind as the businesses you compete with leverage the power of joint venturing to gobble up market share, mind share, and brand share.

Understanding the high volume of joint venture opportunities available today can certainly help you make the paradigm shift. Here are just two examples in the automotive industry that show how very big companies are reaching out to smaller companies and providing support for joint venture efforts.

Toyota's Opportunity Exchange. Each year, Toyota holds its "Opportunity Exchange," a forum designed to provide minority business enterprises (MBEs) across the nation the chance to network and develop relationships with more than 250 of Toyota's suppliers. Toyota's Tier I suppliers, those who supply parts directly to Toyota, attend the event as exhibitors for the purpose of doing more business with minority-owned companies. Toyota estimates that representatives from more than 800 MBEs and small businesses attended in 2003, the 14th year the company has held this event. I've had the opportunity to speak at this event on the topic of joint venturing several times and can personally attest to its effectiveness in bringing together companies that are interested in forming alliances to meet Toyota's needs.

"The role we play in making joint ventures happen is to provide the initial contact and the joining of the relationship between a minority business and one of our Tier 1 suppliers," explains T. Williams of Toyota. "A key part in that is that we know the current suppliers; we've formed relationships with them; we know their business philosophy, so we can introduce them to another supplier with a similar type of interest and similar business philosophy. Then we step back and let the companies work out their deal, because the joint venture has to be one that they can live with and that they can deal with. Together they have to be responsible for maintaining the relationships and making sure they can provide the parts of the quality that we need in the timeframe we need them."

Ford's support of supplier diversity. As part of its Minority Supplier Development Program, Ford Motor Company annually presents Supplier Diversity Development Awards to three suppliers. One of these awards, the Corporate Citizenship Award, is given to the majority Tier 1 supplier with an established and successful supplier diversity development program. Ford has received numerous national awards for its long-standing efforts to assure supplier diversity, including programs it sponsors to bring together its Tier 1 and Tier 2 suppliers.

This is just a snapshot of how corporations actively reach out to encourage their suppliers to work together. Big business is not devoted to these programs solely out of blind idealism. America's corporate giants—as well as the many mid-sized companies that also undertake such efforts—understand that by helping to grow smaller businesses, they help broaden and strengthen the end market for their own products. In addition to this broad economic objective, becoming known as a company that supports minority- and women-owned businesses helps these corporations build and penetrate customer bases in those diverse and rapidly growing markets.

On the government side, two factors are impacting small to mid-sized businesses—one in a good way and one in a bad way. On the negative side of the ledger, the reengineering efforts that took place at the federal government level during the Clinton adminis- tration resulted in the "bundling" of smaller contracts into larger contracts for which only big companies would have the resources to compete. This simplified things for the government by dramat- ically reducing the number of contracts to be let but, at the same time, reduced the number of contracts for which small companies could realistically compete. As a result, teaming with larger com- panies to win a small portion of the now larger contracts has be- come an essential strategy for small businesses wishing to do business with the federal government.

On the positive side of the ledger, on the federal, state, and local levels, governments are requiring more and more that prime contractors use a diverse pool of subcontractors. This required pool of subcontractors includes women-owned businesses, minor- ity-owned businesses, veteran-owned businesses, historically un- derutilized businesses (HUBs), and disabled-owned businesses, as well as businesses that reside in certain geographical locations. If these big prime contractors want to win government contracts, they need to establish connections with these smaller companies to meet the requirements.

In addition to meeting government requirements for diversity in subcontractors, prime contractors realize that they can reduce their costs by partnering with smaller businesses since smaller companies tend to have smaller overhead and reduced operating costs. Such cost savings enable prime contractors to fashion more competitive bids when they're seeking government contracts.

Historical Influences

For a long time now in American business—indeed, in global business—bigger has, for the most part, been considered better. Successive waves of consolidation in many industries have produced a situation in which a handful of giants dominate whole fields of endeavor, leaving progressively less market space for small and mid-sized organizations. This historical trend shows no sign of abating.

Often, the only way small and mid-sized companies can compete is to band together to either aggressively go after a niche market or to create a totally new market that the giants aren't aware of yet, or aren't nimble enough to enter first. Finding the resources to make a legitimate run at a niche market or a brand new market can be daunting for a small business owner. Far better to share the risk—and the potential reward—with another company.

Economic Climate

While the availability of financing from banks and other sources fluctuates with the ups and downs of the national economy, finding money to support a new venture, such as developing a new product, is never easy for a small business owner. In a tight lending market, it can sometimes make much more sense to join with another company on a new venture than to struggle through the process of getting bank financing to go it alone.

Likewise, other economic factors such as rising operating costs and higher business taxes and fees can make joint venturing more attractive to many small and mid-sized businesses. As the basic cost of doing business rises, it becomes imperative to find a way to maximize the value gained from every dollar spent.

The impact of globalization and the ability the Internet has given even the smallest companies to attract customers from far outside their normal geographic market are also driving more companies to joint venturing. Globalization and the Internet open wide vistas of opportunities that many companies aren't ready to take advantage of on their own. Partnering can prove an effective way to make it possible to serve markets far beyond anything previously possible.

As Dan Robinson, manager of Global Purchasing/Market Access at Xerox Corporation, says, "The days are gone when I can stand on the top of my manufacturing plant and say, 'There are all my suppliers; they're within a 15- to 20-mile radius.' Now if I'm a small business and I know that reality exists, I have to start looking into the Far East, Mexico, and Eastern Europe and asking, 'What does it take for me to partner with those companies?'"

Another impact of the global economy is that, with the economic doors open across the world to everyone, American businesses have been forced to lose the arrogance, myopia, and slowness that dominated many sectors of industry in the decades following World War II. We no longer dominate the world's commerce, a fact that forces us to recognize that we cannot make it by ourselves and that joint venturing is a wiser path in many cases.

As I mentioned in the Introduction, one of the economic factors that is driving the growth of joint venturing is downsizing. With many displaced workers deciding that self-employment is the best route for them, they are discovering that they can achieve their business and income goals faster through forming alliances with others who are in a similar position of just starting out on the new road of self-employment.

Societal Events

Societal developments across the world are opening up markets that previously were closed to American businesses. Within recent memory, the possibility of doing business in South Africa, in the nations of Eastern Europe, in the republics of the former Soviet Union, or in China was unthinkable. Now these markets are available to American companies prepared to take advantage of the dramatic shifts that occurred, for example, with the downfall of communism in Eastern Europe or the end of apartheid in South Africa. Here again, taking advantage of these new markets requires being able to operate on a global basis, which, in turn, often is best done through joint venturing. The giant populations of emerging nations such as India and China make these markets extremely attractive to American businesses.

Strategic Alliances = Survival

In an economy and a competitive environment in which every business owner must consistently be at the top of his or her game to survive, joint venturing simply makes sense for many businesses. Being part of a joint venture makes it harder for a competitor to lure away your customers, because the combined resources of two organizations are stronger than the individual resources of one organization.

Every workday, the average small business owner deals with complex production, personnel, customer service, market development, and financing issues. Having a trusted and skilled ally whose interests are closely linked with yours to help generate ideas and solutions to business challenges has never made more sense than it does today.

CROSSING THE AISLE TO SUCCESSFUL JOINT VENTURING

Even though their business fields were closely related and they sat on different sides of the same aisle in church, Michael Sales Sr., and Tim Allston of Huntsville, Alabama, didn't know each other until a fellow church member brought them together for a business opportunity.

Retiring after 26 years in marketing research with Procter & Gamble in Cincinnati, Sales had moved to Huntsville and opened High Impact Marketing in 1999. In 2001, Allston established Allston Communications Inc., a public relations and professional speaking firm. Together, they now operate a joint venture called Smorgasbord Joint Ventures, which offers professional speaking/training, marketing, and public relations services. Here's the story of how they became joint venture partners and their thoughts on what strategic partnering offers entrepreneurs like themselves:

Allston: A church member, Guy Juzang, hired us both as consultants for Infinity Technology, his aerospace engineering company. There, I began to learn of Mike [Sales]'s strengths in marketing, and he learned of my strengths in public relations.

Sales: Infinity Technology asked us to meet together and to handle its PR and marketing. It kind of forced us in a room together, and as we started to talk, we found that our jobs and skills overlapped. Furthermore, as we needed additional resources, we were able to find other entrepreneurs to help us on various project aspects. By the time that initial yearlong contract was over, Tim [Allston] and I had established relationships with four or five different entrepreneurs upon whom we could call. Plus, we all worked well together.

For example, when we needed to get our own Web site designed, we used some of the same people with whom we had been working for this company. We then offered, "Hey, what we can do on our Web site is let you have a link, and vice-versa. If people come here and need marketing, they get even more service offerings—and get it more cost-efficiently—just by coming to our partnership, versus going to just one of us." So we formed sort of a loose partnering relationship with four or five other groups. That gives us an advantage in that we're getting exposure from five Web sites instead of just from one Web site.

Learning on the Job

Allston: Before Mike and I first met, I had recently lost a major IT client; one reason I lost it was because I had tried to do it all by myself. I really thought I could. From that jarring life lesson—an important wake-up call for many early-stage entrepreneurs—humbled, I began to pray, "Lord, what will I do?"

Shortly thereafter, I met Mike, and we began to swap our business "war stories." One day, I shared with him my unique and evolving research about my "ego-holic" addiction and my upcoming book on being an "ego-holic in recovery" entitled, *Are Our Egos Destroying Us? Confessions of a Recovering Ego-holic;* the next time we met, Mike had drawn all these diagrams and these mind-maps on my book and topic—far beyond what and where I was thinking!

I began to see that he knew and envisioned *light-years* more than I knew. The traditional entrepreneur says, "This is my ball"; but I began to see after that one experience that I could probably gain more from and with him than I could on my own.

Soon afterward, I was booked to present a two-hour seminar on being a recovering ego-holic. Mike helped me "rescue" that potentially two-hour talking-head lecture: he coaxed me into inventing a more fun-filled and interactive "Welcome to the Twin Cities of Egos" workshop, which received rave evaluations.

Mike, I later learned, had moderated more than 1,200 workshops and focus groups around the world, and was a trained listener; on the other hand, I'd been a public speaker since age three. I said, "These are two separate worlds." And he said, "Do they have to be?" and I said, "Hmmm, maybe not."

When I was booked to present a two-day time management seminar, it hit me, "Let me tag-team it with this brother. He's probably forgotten more than I'll ever know!" It, too, was a success and has become an annual booking for us now. I realized early on the best way for me to learn what he knows is to go out and get consulting and speaking contracts for us, so we can work together. I can sit at his feet—scotch-taped to him—and learn what he could teach me. I'm the Rap, the business prospector; and he's the Map, the drafter of our proposals and presentations.

Because of our varied, but overlapping strengths, we created and began presenting our unique seminar-workshop format. We came up with the name "Smorgasbord" to visually portray our creation. We said, "Let's create a menu of the hottest topics out there. Clients can pick, buffet-style, several topics, and we will put it together in a part-lecture, part-hands-on workshop/totally fun menu serving." That became the birth of Smorgasbord Seminar-Workshops.

Sales: I didn't start my business thinking about joint venturing. When I started my business and someone asked me, "Mike, you're a marketing person; we really need some key artwork. Can you do that?" That's not my specialty, but I said, "No, I don't do that, but I know someone who does," and I would just give him or her over to that referenced person.

After hearing requests like that repeatedly for a while, I said, "Instead of sending the business to someone else, why don't I say, 'Yes, we can cover that, within High Impact Marketing'? And then I'd go out and find someone for the work, but now under the High Impact umbrella. I'd say to the person, "This is what I'm working on. Are you interesting in working on it with me?" And then after we'd worked a couple of these projects together, we asked ourselves, "Why not do this on a regular basis, so we can help anyone who needs marketing and graphic arts help as well?"

To give an example, Tim and I were hired by a company in Huntsville to do PR work on his side and marketing work on mine. One of our assignments called for us to produce a video. Neither of us are video people, but we joint ventured with a person who was. So the three of us came together on that project and got it done very efficiently. Not only did we save the client money, but we also were able to do it in half the time.

You don't have to have related businesses to joint venture. You could be totally dissimilar businesses but can joint venture on, say, rental space, secretarial help, or accounting services. Companies that are dissimilar can come together and share in those expenses under one roof. A plus to being dissimilar is the automatic cross-fertilization of ideas, best-practices, and industry cultures, all of which bring added value to both the joint venture partners as well as the clients.

What Partners Need from Each Other

Sales: The first thing I would look for in a joint venture partner is integrity and honesty. In conversation, I would find out how they have interacted with people in the past. What kinds of projects have they done? How do they evaluate a particular business situation? Whether they evaluate things primarily on money or they want to build a marquee and want their name up there—those are the kinds of signs that tell me this person may not have the integrity I value.

If they value money more than relationships, that will come out in conversation. If it's a lot of "me, me, me, I'm great, people need to know how great I am," well, those are indicators to me that this might be a person I don't want to do business with.

Allston: I agree wholeheartedly. If you've got integrity, you can build expertise; but it's hard to build integrity if people don't have it in them. I also look for someone who knows more than I do and is smarter than me in order to stretch myself. I believe one has to be willing to be stretched. I have to have the aptitude and willingness to be taught.

What Stops People from Partnering

Sales: Joint venturing may seem obvious, but I think one of the reasons small businesses don't do it more often is that we simply don't know enough about it. We fear what we don't know. Often, I'll sit down with small businesses and people who are starting out, and I'll say things that are obvious to me, and they'll say, "Wow, that's a revelation." It never occurred to them, and nobody before had sat down and told them.

In the African-American community, we don't come from a culture in which dads and mothers were professionals and they were in business and they did deals. We are probably the first generation in our age bracket to ever have that experience, and we're just learning it now in the second half of our careers. Now, our sons and daughters are coming along, and we can teach them, and they'll start looking at opportunities to do things together; but we haven't had a generation to go through it. So it's incumbent on us to pass things along, to create more instances where we can mentor people, and get them exposed to things like joint venturing.

Allston: We come out of a culture in which we were taught to go to school, get an education, get a job, work, get Social Security upon retirement, and then get your gold watch. Little did we realize that there is no real future in that scenario. But in our culture as blacks in business, we have not been encouraged to take that calculated leap of faith called entrepreneurship. So we didn't have a consistent army of entrepreneurial role models that we could touch and feel. We now have to create the aptitude in our people.

Here's another thing that holds people back from joint venturing. It's like being in school. All your life in school you did your homework, read your reading assignments, received your report card, and your diploma had your name on it. All of a sudden you're sent to work in a job, which now tells you, "Here's the team you will work with." And you say, "I didn't get here with a team; why am I working with a team now?" So we have a bunch of Lone Rangers and Wonder Women out here, believing their own press releases! Obviously, I was once there, too.

When you first become an entrepreneur, many times you're looking at it as your chance to be a part of the American Dream. There is a certain sense of rugged American individualism, John Wayne-ism, and Manifest Destiny that we carry into our businesses.

When I had the contract I mentioned earlier with the major IT company, the first thing that came to mind was, "Finally, I'm getting paid for my true genius to show." Well, my "true genius" lost the contract in six weeks. At termination, they told me, "Tim, you needed help; you knew it and we knew it, but you never asked. Losing this contract will be one of the best lessons for you as an early-stage entrepreneur—Why?—because talent is not your problem."

That wake-up call forced me to begin to think along the lines of, "How can I spread this out to get many more folks to buy into my vision, to give me a new vision of some things, and to overcome my warts?"

A lot of what Mike and I do together is by handshake. I'm the one out there doing the business development, not that he can't, but I'm the talker. Because of his wisdom and experience, Mike is drawing the models in his mind while the prospective client is talking. I may never become a model-drawer; I don't have to be. Instead, I now align myself with the model-drawer. So many of us are so concerned with, "If I share this, will I lose something?" I'm learning as an entrepreneur that there is enough pie out here for everybody.

What New Entrepreneurs Should Know

Sales: I would tell young people who want to joint venture to be very mindful of needs. When you're talking with people and they express a need that is not being filled, then start thinking how you can fulfill that need. And if you can't fill it, then ask yourself, Who can? Do you have a friend or know someone else who can?

Get in a habit of looking for needs and asking who can fill them if you can't. That becomes a model in your mind for everything that comes up.

Allston: I once read a quote on a church marquee in Orlando, Florida, that offered, "Coincidence occurs when God chooses to remain anonymous." So believing that, you begin to ask yourself, why did so-and-so contact me? Why did this person come into my path? And you also recognize that if I give of myself I'll get so much more. Don't try to simply hoard opportunities and make blessings only a one-way communication. Help other people understand that every single contact works. Help people acquire the networking opportunities they'll need, because every contact they acquire will become operational in the evolution of time.

Joint venturing makes good business sense. What I'm noticing more and more in the business world is that the big dinosaur-like companies are on their way out. Daniel Pink in his book, *Free Agent Nation,* makes the point that it is the freelancer and the entrepreneur who really are driving the economy.

The idea of Wonder Woman or Superman is gone. We are an amalgamation of people and things, and so I don't have to be an expert on everything anymore. Mike and I do a seminar-workshop on "The 80/20 Principle: How to Achieve More by Doing Less." Twenty percent of what you do yields 80 percent of the results.

I recognize my spiritual gifts are in public speaking, educating, encouraging, and networking. I do write for a living, but if someone else can write better or faster, let me farm that out to them; this mindset helps to create a whole new class of entrepreneurs.

The near future will showcase a wider range of joint venturing; and we're going to see joint venturing in which people may never see each other. There will be some e-hub of being able to come together; companies coming together that might not see each other but are joined by a relationship—an electronic relationship, a spiritual relationship, a professional relationship, leading to potentially entrepreneurial relationships. The possibilities are only limited by our imagination.

ENCOURAGING SUPPLIER ALLIANCES AT PROCTER & GAMBLE

Procter & Gamble markets almost 300 products to more than five billion consumers in 140 countries. The company has more than 98,000 employees. One of them is Icy Williams, who serves as associate director of Supplier Diversity Development. At P&G, the bar is set very high in terms of the company's efforts to support the growth of smaller businesses owned by minorities and women; the company's Supplier Diversity Network is made up of approximately 1,200 businesses, with which P&G will spend 11 percent of its procurement budget in 2005. That 11 percent represents an annual target of $1.5 billion. In this interview, Williams talks about the role joint venturing plays in helping the consumer packaged goods colossus achieve its Supplier Diversity Development goal.

What role does joint venturing play in your work with minority- and women-owned businesses?

Williams: P&G has been playing in this arena for quite some time. We have caused quite a few joint ventures, acquisitions, or alliances to take place. My own experience with this is through the relationships I continue to develop with minority- and women-owned firms that we recognize are capable and have the capacity to play in fields where we don't yet have supplier diversity, such as the chemical arena, the major large warehousing arena, the original equipment manufacturers, or the substrate areas.

We believe that by getting to know these companies, we can find ways to bring them in when opportunities arise. All of the Supplier Diversity managers must stay on top of things because if we don't, opportunities that become available internally can quickly pass by before we get a chance to make the smaller companies aware of them.

In other cases, we have identified areas in which we don't have Supplier Diversity Development, and we have developed tactical plans to get more diversity in those areas. We're in the midst right now of looking at how we can create an opportunity for an MBE in the whole non-woven substrate area. Within the business unit, a purchasing associate director believed in this enough to say we're going to work with our majority supplier to find and develop one for this area. Those are the kinds of things that occur because of our supplier diversity strategies.

P&G is not a joint venture partner, but we may look at our majority suppliers and say, "We want you to bring an MBE option in with you because we're doing a major amount of business with you." Our belief is that if we don't play a major role in making that happen, we'll not achieve our results. Because of Supplier Diversity Development efforts, it's important for us to find ways to help make networking linkages happen, either through our own knowledge transfer or through the education of our suppliers.

Of the alliances you've helped facilitate, what are your thoughts about why some have worked and others didn't?

Williams: In the alliances that have worked, there have been a number of elements to create wins on both sides. First, it's important that a diverse supplier comes to us with a competitive advantage who has the capacity and capability, who is already in this business, who knows it well and considers the work part of its core competence. Second, the alliance partners having a strong relationship prior to this project have the best success over time. When this relationship is in place, then P&G is not only there for the front end, but there throughout the entire process. We continue to leverage that alliance, and we look at how we include them in our supply chain. It is important that we coach and develop the alliance so that we don't always just keep them in the competitive process side of our purchasing matrix model. P&G looks for ways to move alliances along that matrix and as the alliance grows and develops, they then start to be looked at as more of a key alliance in our supply chain. Alliances with these types of elements are the ones that work well and continue to work well.

What about the alliances that don't work? What happens there?

Williams: The alliances that do not work sometimes are just the opposite of those that do work. On one hand the M/WBEs too quickly form an alliance without doing all of the due diligence necessary to create a good working relationship. Other times, when P&G doesn't foster the kind of business relationship that says, "I'm holding you, large majority supplier, responsible for this relationship," then the alliances usually will have problems of customer ownership throughout the project.

In addition, when the diverse supplier hiccups, and they will, we sometimes don't hold that majority supplier responsible for cleaning up the issues the majority supplier created in the alliance relationship. Again, I think it's because of how we think about the diverse supplier in our supply chain versus the majority supplier:

- Do we think about them as being important/critical to our business?
- Do we manage and work with diverse suppliers like we do with our majority suppliers?
- What kind of follow-up do we do with them?
- What kind of coaching do we do with them?
- What kind of advice do we offer?

When many of the points listed above are not addressed on the front end of these alliances, then the minority-owned company tends to be seen as the problem if an alliance goes bad.

What about situations in which you've seen or facilitated minority firms joining together to bid on big contracts?

Williams: I have not seen this happen the way I would like to see it. I think this is critical development work that needs to happen. Globalization is driving us to find capable diverse companies joining together in consortiums to go after big business awards. I've only had one discussion on this topic since I've been in this role; there was one group that I brought together to talk about the concept. They were open to it. I asked the question of why they hadn't done this in the past, and there were a whole lot of reasons, but it's really about this thing of control. And that gets to be the biggest issue as to why they can't come together; it's this idea of losing control.

As P&G continues to globalize and leverage itself with companies that can bring a competitive advantage, minority- and women-owned businesses will need to continuously think about different ways to come after our business, because they can't keep coming to us as small mom-and-pops. If they come in consortiums that are large enough to compete, they have as good a chance to win the business as anybody else. But that means giving up a piece of that control to the partners.

Some people say that large corporations look at a couple of minority firms coming together as riskier or possibly offering less value

than if a majority-owned firm and a minority-owned firm come together. Do you think that view is valid?

Williams: I think that has some validity because when a smaller company joins with a larger company, they're usually looking for something they don't have. Most of the time it is either a capital infusion or the front end of something associated with the product or service. Oftentimes it's the research capability; most small companies don't have that technical piece of research and development.

I can't speak for others, but having that front-end technical capability clearly adds a totally different look when I'm looking at a smaller company for product manufacturing. But there are some fields in which that's not a barrier, such as construction, or staffing and personnel, or even IT. In those arenas, two smaller companies can easily come together and bring a competitive advantage to a large corporation's business needs.

What is P&G willing to do to facilitate the strategy of acquisition when you have a minority business purchasing a majority business?

Williams: The best story we have is in the whole area of cartons. We facilitated an MBE acquiring two majority companies, and it's been because of the people at P&G who had a passion and commitment for supplier diversity development. At the beginning of the process, P&G knew that the sale was going on with one of our majority suppliers. So we ensured that the MBE was in the mix for the discussion with the majority company and made sure that whoever was managing that sale knew about the MBE. Then we helped to facilitate introductions and ensured that people knew how this MBE was playing a role in the P&G supply chain.

What characteristics do the majority companies that seem more likely to engage in joint ventures tend to have?

Williams: They tend to show up as we do in the supplier diversity area:

- Leadership commitment
- Dedicated resources
- Goals/targets/measures with action plans
- Scorecard reviews with leadership
- Reward and recognition systems supporting supplier diversity development

In addition, they come to us with ideas around how they can potentially play in this arena with us.

What advice would you give to minority- or women-owned firms about joint venturing?

Williams: I would advise them to take the time and do their homework. Their homework has to be focused on where they want to play in this changing world. They need to assess their organization's capacities and abilities around where they want to play. If they want to grow, then they need to figure out what the right model is. Is it joint venturing, is it acquisition, is it some strategic alliance? They need to do the strategic business planning that clearly indicates where they stand with the corporation today—their current state. They need to plan their future state—with clearly defined objectives, goals, strategies, and measures—that shows a joint venture is the option that is going to take them to the next level, or the fifth level, that they want to achieve.

In that self-assessment, they may have to do some education around what a joint venture will do for them versus an acquisition, or what this strategic alliance will do for them versus a joint venture. I think they need to do that kind of homework instead of just diving in when some Fortune 500 company or majority supplier says, "I've got this joint venture opportunity for you."

What would you say to majority firms?

Williams: P&G's base expectation is that majority suppliers are going to help us meet our supplier diversity goals and objectives. We aggressively work with majority suppliers on their supplier diversity programs and encourage and train them on how incorporating minorities and women in their plans helps P&G with our supplier diversity goals. Their incentive for doing that could be continuing to do business with P&G in the long term. We will continue to do supplier diversity, and we will continue to accelerate opportunities to do more spending. So for majority companies, it's a matter of how do they continue to win with P&G as they help us achieve our goals and our objectives.

Joint ventures are not for everybody. Whether it's majority companies or women- and minority-owned companies, don't just jump into joint ventures. Really seek out people who have been doing it, people who are experienced, people who can coach, and people who can get you through that process. I think it's very important for companies to be educated in this arena. Joint ventures are major, major decisions. It's like the first time you buy a house; it's like getting married; these are major life-changing decisions in individuals' lives and you can't just haphazardly go into a relationship like that. So I can't reinforce this point enough: if you're going to play in this field, be educated, and then you can make conscious choices versus unconscious choices.

3

THE STRATEGIC PARTNERSHIP MODEL

A Roadmap for a Successful Joint Venture

"Alone we can do so little: together we can do so much."
HELEN KELLER

The majority of entrepreneurs struggle with how to initiate, build, and maintain a successful joint venture. I jokingly remind people in my workshops that joint venturing is like teen sex. Everyone says they're doing it; but half of them are lying, and of the half who aren't, most of them don't do it especially well. The same holds true for most businesses that seek to build alliances with other businesses.

It is easy to understand why most businesses struggle with constructing effective joint ventures and strategic alliances because such partnerships by nature tend to be very complex undertakings. My engineering background and training taught me that the best way to solve a complex problem is to first break it into smaller, manageable components. Then arrange the components in such a way that together they create a working model that is simple, easy to implement, repeatable, and reliable. As I attempted to master the art of forming business alliances, I decided to follow my own advice and developed what I believe is a good working model, or map, that outlines the necessary steps entrepreneurs need to take to build effective joint ventures.

Having a map to follow, especially the first time you journey into joint venture territory, is extremely advisable. My Strategic Partnership Model will help you understand all the things you need to do to establish your joint venture on firm footing. This model is based upon more than 20 years of research, interviews, anecdotal experiences, and observation of entrepreneurs who have struggled (some successfully and others not so successfully) with this task.

Reginald K. Layton is Diversity Business Development Director at Johnson Controls, Inc., in Milwaukee, Wisconsin. Johnson Controls, Inc., a $22.8 billion company, employs 115,000 people worldwide and is one of the most successful suppliers to the automotive industry. In a discussion I had with him, he confirmed the value of having a model to follow. Layton stated:

> From my observation, successful joint ventures are dependent on the execution of the proper sequence of events. For example, the first step in building successful joint ventures is relationship building. Relationship building is then followed by the leadership of the two companies coming to an agreement on what the project mechanics and structure of the relationship will look like. Once executive agreement on the structure of the deal is completed, then the real work of the companies' legal counsel begins by structuring the legal framework that will allow the business relationship to flourish.

In this chapter, I'll provide an overview of my Strategic Partnership Model so you get a sense of the overall flow of the joint venture development process. (See Figure 3.1.) Then, each phase will be discussed in detail in coming chapters.

FIGURE 3.1 *The Strategic Partnership Model*

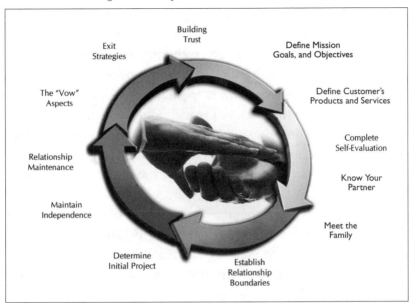

Building
Trust

Exit
Strategies

Define Mission
Goals, and Objectives

The "Vow"
Aspects

Define Customer's
Products and Services

Complete
Self-Evaluation

Relationship
Maintenance

Know Your
Partner

Maintain
Independence

Meet the
Family

Determine
Initial Project

Establish
Relationship
Boundaries

THE STRATEGIC PARTNERSHIP MODEL

Building trust. Although lots of tasks can get accomplished between two or more companies looking to form alliances, very little of real substance or positive value can be created unless the people within the organizations share a bond of trust and mutual respect. Building trust is a delicate issue that becomes even more challenging when the people who are considering a partnership are different. Differences can be defined and sliced by class, culture, gender, race, ethnicity, geography, and other criteria. As I will discuss in Chapter 4, by being aware of the differing attitudes of people who are on the other side of the racial, ethnic, or gender divide, you are better prepared to overcome common misperceptions and build the trust that will be the bedrock of your joint venture.

Define mission, goals, and objectives. The major benefit of creating a strategic alliance is that the alliance allows all companies involved to compete for an opportunity that neither company alone could realize. Opportunity gaps or vacuums develop in markets due to uncertainty, chaos, inconsistencies, timing, lags, or leads in market developments, technological evolution (or revolution), and/or inertia. Going after these opportunities in the market often requires adding new skills to a company, and the quickest way to do this may be through joint venturing. Entrepreneurs who recognize these opportunity gaps or vacuums before competitors do can identify potential partners to help them assemble the best team possible to go after the newly emergent market opportunity.

Bringing this team together successfully requires that each potential alliance member is crystal clear on the joint venture's mission (the scope of the venture and the dominant emphasis and values), goals (usually quantitative targets, such as to increase market share by 15 percent or increase revenues by 25 percent—though sometimes qualitative, such as improving customer service or improving the quality of existing products or services), and objectives.

Never be tempted to skip or rush through this important strategic planning exercise without giving it ample attention. By being very explicit about what you hope to achieve together up front, you and your prospective partner can avoid huge problems down the road.

Define customers, products, and services. After you've established your joint venture's mission, the next step is to identify your target customers and which products and services these customers will be offered. Determining which customer or customers you need to focus on and what it is that you collectively bring to the table (products and/or services) will maximize your efficiencies as a team and minimize duplicating work. Again, because you are working with a partner who may have a different set of customers and different ideas about what the products or services should be, this can be an intricate decision-making process.

Complete self-evaluation. Shakespeare said, "To thine own self be true." This adage couldn't be more important than in the consummation of a joint venture. As you work with your potential partner to define the mission, goals, and objectives, and identify the customers and products or services, you also should give your own organization a thorough analysis to determine if you have the capabilities needed to fulfill your part in this proposed joint venture. Part of this self-analysis involves asking yourself one important question: "What value do I bring to this team that my partner either does not have or, if she has it, doesn't do as well as I do?" Another question you might want to ask yourself is, "Could this team be successful if I were not on it?" This type of self-evaluation helps you to position your role on the team and what value you bring.

This self-evaluation process cannot be fully completed until specifics of the joint venture are determined, because until you understand what will be required of your company, you can't determine whether your organization has the "right stuff" for this particular joint venture. However, there is much analysis you can do in parallel with the mission definition step so you are ready to say yes or no to the partnership at the appropriate time.

Know your partner. Just as it's important to know your own organization thoroughly before entering into a joint venture, you definitely need to know all about the organization you're considering as a partner. I am still amazed at the number of companies that fail to exercise proper due diligence in researching and studying potential partners. You could be putting your company on the line by aligning with another firm. Isn't your company worth a little extra effort and time up front to protect it from the dangers of a bad partnership?

Meet the parents. My wife of 26 years and I met at the University of Pennsylvania School of Engineering. Yes, it was love at first sight, and after a very intense and wonderful courtship, I concluded that I wanted her to be my bride. But before I was willing to tie the knot, I had a burning desire to first meet her parents. Although young, I understood that when you marry someone, you not only marry her, but you marry the entire family—including the good, the bad, and the ugly. Luckily for me, I did my homework on the parents and family and ended up marrying into a wonderful family.

Some businesses, though, are not so lucky, because they fail to dig deeper into their potential partners' character and past. The parents and family are defined as any person, organization, or institution that directly or indirectly interfaces with the company with which you are proposing to create an alliance. These entities could include employees, stockholders, vendors, government officials, trade leaders, and competitors. The health of your alliance will depend on many people who will not be in the room when the partnership is being formed. The last thing you want to have happen is to find out after you've inked a deal that key employees in your partner's organization aren't up to getting the job done or that your partner has bad relationships with vendors who are essential to making the joint venture a success. This is why it's essential to take time to get to know the family up front.

Establish relationship boundaries. Setting boundaries for the relationship is essential. This includes determining up front what your process will be for resolving the conflicts that inevitably arise in any partnership. By having this discussion before anything goes amiss, you will assure that problems get ironed out quickly with less possibility of causing any animosity between the two sides.

Determine first-step project. Nothing happens until something happens! This may sound like a Yogi Berra-ism, but it really drives home the point that good intentions and stellar joint venture legal documents won't measure up to a hill of beans until the joint venture team begins working on a first-step project. Even if the initial project is small, you want it to be well defined. Both partners must be crystal clear about things like the project plan, timeline, performance measures, and financial commitments before moving forward.

Maintain independence. Unless you are planning to completely integrate your company with another company, you must maintain a certain level of independence from your partner so your company can continue to grow and prosper beyond the joint venture's end point. By being clear up front on which assets are part of the deal and which are not, you will avoid misunderstandings and be able to properly leverage your other assets, customers, and opportunities to benefit your company in other ways.

Another reason for maintaining independence is that, depending on the size of your joint venture, you could risk being distracted from your existing business, especially at a very critical time. It's important that mechanisms are in place to assure that your current product line or services receive the necessary continued support. This includes communicating clearly about the joint venture with your current customers, vendors, and other stakeholders so they know exactly how this new undertaking will affect your ongoing business.

Relationship maintenance. I often warn my clients that if your business isn't growing, then it is dying. Some will argue that if it has reached steady state, that is a good place to be. Our business environment is constantly changing and consolidating, so adjustment to that dynamic requires that businesses scale quickly and efficiently to at least maintain their positions in the marketplace. Likewise with maintaining joint venture relationships—if the relationship isn't growing, then it is dying. Just because the deal is signed doesn't mean your work is done. As with any relationship, it will require constant monitoring and maintenance. You must continually take the temperature of the relationship to make sure that everything is well.

Blood vows—legal aspects of joint ventures. Joint ventures come in many legal forms. While a lot of this can be left to the lawyers, there are legal issues you need to understand and decisions you need to make before signing on the dotted line. I put this information toward the end of the model not because it actually occurs at the end, but because it's rather dry information. However, never forget that it is also critical information, so please don't skip this chapter when you come to it.

Exit strategies. Like everything else in life, all good things must come to an end, including joint ventures. The exit strategy defines how the entrepreneurs will bring the alliance to an orderly and scheduled close. The same amount of effort that goes into building a joint venture/alliance should go into developing workable strategies for exiting. How are you going to dissolve this thing when the mission is achieved? How will you bring the relationship to a close in such a way that all parties involved feel good about the experience and that they are walking away a better company than before they engaged in the alliance? The choices for exiting are many, but they need to be determined from the very start so that there are no misunderstandings when the partnership nears the end of its days.

HOW THE MODEL HELPS

Whenever I speak with entrepreneurs who want to pursue a joint venture opportunity, the biggest complaint I hear is that they have no roadmap for putting the deal together. They possess no step-by-step method that will guide them through this rigorous, confusing, and sometimes frightening process. A primary goal for my Strategic Partnership Model is to provide this much-needed step-by-step methodology and to encourage business owners to be more analytical when approaching joint ventures. There is a tendency among businesses both large and small not to do their homework before entering into joint ventures. This homework, as the model shows, includes evaluating your own organization and its partnering goals and capabilities; it also includes closely scrutinizing your prospective partner to make sure that good alignment exists between the two organizations.

The dynamics of the joint venture model take an interesting twist when the relationship is between a small company and a large corporation. Oftentimes for a small business, this type of business relationship is a "do or die" type of arrangement. The small business, seeking to either grow or just simply survive, will more times than not commit a higher percentage of its corporate resources to working the deal than the large company will. Most small businesses will have very little room for error. Besides, unless there is a long-term relationship between the two companies, the large corporation will often use the leverage of bringing another small business into the deal to apply pressure to the small business and to win concessions.

With more "skin in the game," the small business often will feel it has very little choice but to concede to terms and conditions to which it normally would not agree. Depending on the size of the joint venture, a small business owner could, in fact, be putting his or her company's future on the line. It is, therefore, critical to move through all the steps of the Strategic Partnership Model to ensure that you make the right choice in partners and that the joint venture is structured to protect your company's interests and safeguard its future.

Following the Strategic Partnership Model also helps ensure that you won't leap into a possibly ill-conceived joint venture merely because you're flattered to be asked to do so by a large corporation. When an important customer or another big, impressive organization contacts you about the possibility of a joint venture, it is easy to be so excited about just being asked to the party that you don't take the time to reflect upon whether this is actually a good idea. Following the Strategic Partnership Model will help you keep your emotional reactions to the idea of partnering with someone big under control.

Another important thing this Strategic Partnership Model does is prompt you to be proactive rather than reactive in the joint venture process. There are certain events that you know will happen. The venture will begin and it will end. Each company will be changed by the experience and will never be the same. There will be disagreements and conflict between the partners. For example, it makes sense to establish a conflict-resolution process at the beginning of the relationship. This process, agreed upon while sane minds are prevailing, will establish a way to overcome problems that arise later. In addition, you will learn more about the culture of your prospective partner's organization as you discuss potential conflict-resolution options. Thus, by being proactive, you will accomplish two important goals that you wouldn't have achieved if you simply sat back and waited for something to go wrong and then reacted to it.

As I stressed earlier, there is no reason you have to sit back and wait for a potential joint venture partner to call you. By knowing the steps you will need to take as you move toward establishing a partnership, you will be more self-assured about picking up the phone and making that initial phone call.

C a s e   S t u d y

BUILDING SUPPLIERS WHILE BUILDING AUTOS AT FORD MOTOR COMPANY

Since 1987, Ray Jensen has been in a perfect position to observe and facilitate joint ventures and strategic alliances. As director of Ford Motor Company's Supplier Diversity Development Program, Ray has led a program that has won numerous national and regional awards for its effectiveness in developing opportunities for minority suppliers to do business with the automotive giant. Part of that success has been the company's ability to foster strategic alliances in the minority community. Jensen estimates he's witnessed at least 20 or more joint ventures. He readily admits that the company has made mistakes but also confirms that Ford has learned a lot about how supplier partnerships should work. Here, Jensen talks about what he has learned over the years about strategic alliances.

What is Ford's interest in helping companies do joint ventures?

Jensen: Ford has $150 billion in annual revenues and 330,000 employees around the world. Our suppliers are basically publicly traded companies with revenues of hundreds of millions of dollars; some are billion-dollar companies. We do business with large suppliers; that's the natural order of Ford Motor Company and the entire automotive industry.

We have this unique ability, which most major corporations don't have, to build and develop large suppliers and establish long-term relationships with them. Because we have the capability, it would be unconscionable for us not to leverage it to work for the unique area we're operating in. We can't change suppliers like we change underwear.

Once we get a supplier, it's like a marriage, and we stick together until death do us part. It takes two to three years to go from the concept of a vehicle to when it rolls off the assembly line, and 54 percent of the parts in that vehicle are made in-house, but 46 percent of the parts come from suppliers. So our suppliers better be healthy and able to deliver, and that requires development. When we need a part, we cannot afford a supplier who can't deliver, because that may shut down the assembly line.

Large suppliers, we have felt, are more stable than small suppliers. If you can have a downturn for three or four years and don't have the critical mass to sustain yourself over that time, you're going to be out of business. So it is imperative that our suppliers be large and growing, and we know minority suppliers have not had the longevity of some of our majority suppliers.

For minority suppliers to come up to the point where they can compete successfully, they have to go through joint ventures and acquisitions. They're probably not going to achieve the size Ford needs through the regular organic growth. Therefore, we recognize that a part of our development process is to look for amenable, meaningful joint ventures and acquisitions.

What are some of the lessons you've learned over the years about joint ventures?

Jensen: A joint venture has to be one that is sustaining. If a minority-owned company is involved, it must have the technology. One of the mistakes we've seen time and again is that a majority-owned company goes out and finds a minority company to complement what it does, but the complementary part is not the technology. When that venture is put together, the majority company usually dominates the negotiations and the relationship. The value added by the minority company may be minimal, so that company is like the tail on the dog; it doesn't have the technology to *be* the dog.

When you need capital, people invest in the technology. If the minority firm has the technology, they can attract the capital; then they can be in the position of negotiating the contract. I don't say they can't joint venture with a majority company, but they have to bring something that has value more than just their minority status. And through that value they control the finances and the business.

Another reason lopsided joint ventures happen is because the customer feels comfortable with the majority company; if the smaller company fails to deliver, the majority company can just take over and deliver the goods. My job for the last two years has been to review each of our joint ventures and look at the value-add the minority brings to the venture. We want to see if the minority, with time, will rule the nest. That's what we look for in joint ventures; with that we're going to create wealth, and we're going to create capable suppliers who can compete.

Now we'll outsource a capability that we've been doing in-house, and if it is going to be outsourced to a minority venture, we ask the minority firm to find a majority partner. We say: "You have the technology, we feel you can do it. You go find a majority partner and come back to us." In the past it was the other way around. So that's the new Ford. We can do that because we have a strong infrastructure to help our suppliers develop in areas such as engineering and technical teams. We have lean manufacturing that we offer to our minority suppliers; we have shadowing where a minority supplier shadows our engineering people; we have technical assistance where we contract with retired automotive types to come in and solve particular problems, and once that problem is solved, we pay 75 percent of the cost of the consultant. We have retirees who have a lot of experience and who have seen problems that minority suppliers are facing. What better way to use these guys than to have them come back and assist. That helps us because we don't have to use our internal resources and hiring these guys creates opportunities for them. The minority and majority partners love it, and it's a win-win. And that's how we nurture these ventures.

How do you determine which companies may be good candidates for joint ventures?

Jensen: We focus on those that meet the criteria for growth, have the right management team in place, and have the product. We're looking for companies that have products and services that are pediatric rather than geriatric; that is, they have products that have the ability to grow and have not matured.

They must have the technology, the thing that is the core competency of that particular business. If they do, then the venture has at least a 50-50 chance of succeeding, because Ford will come forward and help them succeed. We've got to be the fertilizer that grows this venture to make it profitable. We have to be willing to not only put the resources there, as far as sourcing opportunities, but also be willing to put some of the expertise there.

A lot of time small businesses don't have the financial controls in place; they don't have a chief financial officer. We will actually hire a CFO to work for six months and train people to understand the value of strong economic procedures and controls. That's part of the fertilizer we put on these ventures. We also help them take advantage of empowerment zone opportunities by having our Ford Land Development Corporation be involved in the acquisition of property. Ford Land would buy property and lease it back for a nominal fee for four or five years until a company is up and running, and then we actually sell it to them.

Have you seen a difference between two small companies trying to do a joint venture and a large company trying to team with a small company?

Jensen: One difference is you have egos; that's the biggest problem when you have two small companies trying to come together. But we have pulled it off. Not only have we had two companies, we've had three companies form what is called TriTech, which designs and builds paint systems for our plants. One firm is owned by an East Indian who provides architectural design services; one is an African-American firm in construction; and the other one is an Hispanic steel firm. They formed a joint venture that worked together under TriTech competing with a majority supplier.

What do you tell small/minority/women-owed businesses that want to pursue an alliance?

Jensen: Do it for the right reasons. Do it because you gain expertise that you don't have, as long as you have the core competency. If you don't have the core competence, forget it. Don't go into business with someone with the core competency, because that company will dictate the outcome of your success. Second, join a venture for longevity and growth. If the venture isn't going to allow you to grow, then you will lose in the end.

You want to do a joint venture because it's going to give you opportunities you wouldn't have had going it alone. One of the biggest advantages of a joint venture is time to grow; you can move faster because you don't have to reinvent the wheel and you complement each other.

How important is trust in a joint venture?

Jensen: Trust only comes when the business makes sense. Don't do it on trust alone, because the thing that really keeps the venture together is business imperatives. Business is the overwhelming reason for you to be in the joint venture. I wouldn't do it on trust; I would do it on the business proposition that makes sense, and the trust will follow. So it's not, "I trust him so therefore I'm going to give away the store." You need checks and balances.

Do your big suppliers understand why it's in their interest to partner with smaller companies?

Jensen: Yes, they do. But sometimes they argue that supplier development really doesn't affect them; they sell to Ford as a major customer and don't deal with the public. They may not deal with the minority community and don't see a direct benefit of doing so. We say: "If you can offer your customers low cost and a higher quality, doesn't that make you more competitive? Do you know what minorities bring if you give them a chance? They are probably better suppliers than the guys you've been dealing with all these years. They probably have more expertise; these guys have gone to the best business schools in the world and have trained in some of the best corporations. They're nimble and will provide you with cost savings you won't believe. And cost savings make you more competitive. Now who do you think Ford will do business with if we can get a 50 percent cost reduction for the same part?" That's the message I tell them.

4

TRUST: IT MUST BE A TWO-WAY STREET

". . . never to vary a hair's breadth from the truth nor from the path of strictest honesty and honor, with perfect confidence in the wisdom of doing right as the surest means of achieving success . . . . to the maxim that honesty is the best policy should be added another: that altruism is the highest form of egoism as a principle of conduct to be followed by those who strive for success and happiness in public or business relations as well as those of private life."

FROM AN OCTOBER 1904 LETTER BY MR. EDWARD TUCK, WHOSE GIFT PROVIDED FOR THE ESTABLISHMENT OF THE AMOS TUCK SCHOOL OF BUSINESS ADMINISTRATION AT DARTMOUTH COLLEGE

Mutual trust is an essential component of successful joint ventures. When you enter into a joint venture, you are—to some degree or another—putting the fate of your business in another's hands. If your partnership involves only a tiny portion of your business, the risk you're taking is probably not great. Many joint ventures do, in fact, start out with small projects designed for completion within a short time frame, at which point the relationship dissolves. But the possibility also exists that your joint venture will grow over time, or it may even start out as a fairly important part of your business. In such cases, your company's future may depend on the success—or failure—of the joint venture. The need for mutual trust in such a relationship is abundantly clear. You simply cannot afford to enter into a joint venture if trust does not initially exist between the two parties.

At Xerox, Dan Robinson spends from 70 to 80 percent of his time supporting the creation of joint ventures to increase the diversity of the company's supplier base. As he puts it: "Making alliances work is all about the chemistry; it's the soft things. Do I trust you? How about your integrity? Once you remove the chemistry issue, then you have no problems. You can move onto issues like how do we do the financing, how do we structure something technically, or how do we do operations. If I can get that relationship with the chemistry in place, I know we've got a partnership that can clearly deliver on our objectives."

If any doubt exists in your mind about your potential partner's trustworthiness, you need to explore the source of those misgivings. If you are unable to overcome your concerns, after repeated attempts to allay them, then my advice is to trust what your intuition is telling you and back away from the deal.

In many cases, by opening up a dialogue in which both sides are encouraged to bring forth their concerns about the other, you can clear up misunderstandings and misperceptions and move the partnership forward. The honesty and openness required in such a dialogue are two of the key ingredients of trust.

METHODS AND MODELS FOR BUILDING TRUST

Most people intuitively understand the role trust plays in building any type of relationship, let alone a business relationship. As we begin to open ourselves up to other people and entities, we are often concerned about being hurt, embarrassed, or exposed. There are positive sides to our businesses that we don't mind sharing with the world, but there are also not so positive things about our organizations that we would rather not share. To build a lasting and fruitful business relationship, we must be willing to take personal and business risks, including putting all essential issues on the table for review by the other party.

FIGURE 4.1 *The Trust-building Model*

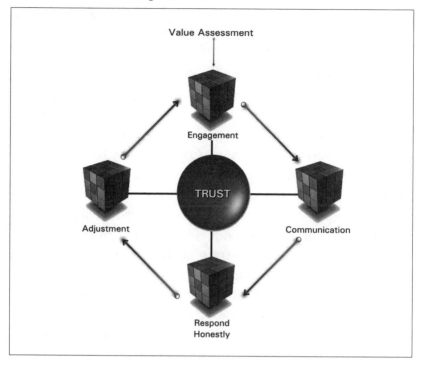

In years of helping businesses (others as well as my own) to engage in joint ventures and strategic alliances, I have adapted two models that work well in helping entrepreneurs build trust among themselves.

THE TRUST-BUILDING MODEL

Here are descriptions of the critical steps illustrated in this model (see Figure 4.1); following these steps will help you build trust with prospective partners.

Values and Gut Assessment

It does not make any sense to join with someone whose values do not match your own. I lecture my children about "marrying well." By this, I am not suggesting that they find someone with loads of money, power, and prestige (although that would be nice) but rather instructing them on the importance of marrying someone you can live with and enjoy for who they are because that will make a good relationship last.

A potential joint venture partner's values leave a trail and your gut (i.e., instinct, intuition, etc.) will readily pick it up like radar picks up incoming aircraft. Look for the "value trail" by listening carefully to how the leadership of the company talks. Observe how they act in certain situations. Consider how they spend their free time and how they carry themselves when no one is around and people aren't looking.

For example, if your potential partner relishes telling you stories of how he or she got vendors to cut their prices by falsely claiming to have lower bids from other vendors, that tells you something about the individual's level of honesty and sense of fair play. What it tells you will, to some degree, be interpreted by your own value system. If, for example, you too enjoy getting the better of vendors and find nothing wrong with it, then you will probably have no problem with this individual.

Process Engagement

As I mentioned in Chapter 3, I am fond of saying that "nothing happens until something happens." The only way we can nurture relationships and build trust is to engage other people. We have to force ourselves to do things with these people—share meals, enjoy recreation together, have the families meet, share each other's burdens and successes, and be a part of each other's lives. Only through process engagement can we collect enough information about the prospective partner and give enough information about ourselves to that partner that we are able to process the reality of the deal. Engaging with each other enables us to begin to make logical and valuable decisions about the relationship and accelerates us on the path to building trust.

Communication

Communication that allows you to offer intimate and detailed information about yourself and your organization and, at the same time, collect similar input from a prospective partner is a crucial mechanism for building trust. Communications among companies is often a difficult process because, as entrepreneurs, we are trained to highlight the good that we do and minimize the bad. We do this as a form of protection for ourselves, our employees, and our company. However, true partnerships and alliances require that we take reasonable risks. Discussing your company objectively—warts and all—is one of the risks that must be accepted to build trust.

I have found that usually in a situation where two companies are considering a joint venture, one of the parties has to have the courage to start sharing information. Someone has to have the foresight to make the first move to divulge confidential facts. What happens beyond that point is very predictable. Sir Isaac Newton formulated in one of his laws of motion that "for every action there is an equal and opposite reaction." This law also applies to human interaction—if you open up, your potential partner will typically respond in kind. The more information you give, the more information she will want to give back. The more intimate information about yourself that you divulge, the more intimate will be the details he is willing to offer.

As the two companies continue to do more and more information sharing, the walls of fear and uncertainty will come tumbling down. If you find yourself in a situation where you are doing all of the giving and the other company is doing all of the taking, then my advice would be to reconsider this relationship.

THE KNOW YOURSELF MODEL

The second model I like to use is what I call the Know Yourself Model. This tool is used to help companies facilitate the com-

FIGURE 4.2 *The Know Yourself Model*

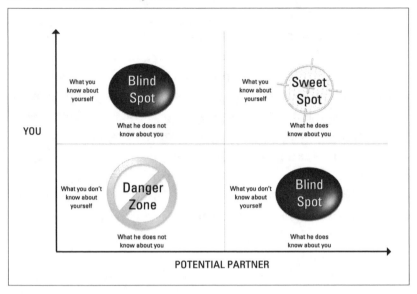

munications and feedback process between themselves and is adapted from the Jo-Harry Window group process model. Typically when two companies are considering an alliance of some type, during the get-to-know-you phase, there are things about each other that are known and things that are not known, as illustrated in Figure 4.2.

On the Y axis, we have you. As shown by the quadrant above, there are things you know about yourself (the upper hemisphere) and things you don't know about yourself (the lower hemisphere). Conversely, on the X axis, we have your potential partner. In the left column are those things about you that your potential partner does not know (e.g., bankruptcy, internal fighting, cash drain, brain drain). In the right column are things about you that the potential partner does know (e.g., customer set, D&B rating, reputation in the industry).

When you start sharing with each other the information that only you know about your companies, the foundation for trust begins building. However, the truly big opportunity for building trust and a long-term relationship lies in the lower right hand quadrant, which contains information your potential partner knows about your company that even you don't know.

For example, you might think your company's performance on a particular contract has been outstanding. Your potential partner might know, based on his contacts with your customer, that the customer is actually so unhappy with the performance that they are looking to remove your firm and "badge swap" your employees with a competitor's staff.

The fact is that as entrepreneurs, our perceptions of our standing in our market and in our industry sometimes differ from the views of our competitors and even our customers. Certainly, your goal should be to have your self-perception of your company match its public perception. The only way to accurately gauge how your organization is viewed by those on the outside is to open yourself up, initiate honest communication with those around you, accept, receive, and believe the feedback you are given, and to passionately and earnestly do something constructive with it, even if it hurts.

A prospective joint venture partner who is willing to share this kind of information with you can be invaluable. If you respond to this feedback in a positive manner, trust will grow on both sides. You will know you can trust your partner to "tell it like it is," and your partner will know he doesn't have to hide bad news from you.

Responding Honestly

Trust building is a contact sport. It requires that you get close to people and organizations, and it dictates that you pay deliberate attention to the feedback your partners provide. Recognize that the relationship will continually change over time, and often that change will be driven by the feedback you receive and the way you respond to that feedback. A positive response on your part will usually help the relationship move forward; a negative, defensive response will slow things down or, in drastic cases, may even bring things to a halt altogether.

Soliciting feedback from a partner on how your actions and behavior affect both the partner and the customer makes it possible to adjust your attitude, processes, and procedures in such a way that the joint venture becomes energized, empowered, and enabled. When you take the time to hear the feedback and act upon it, you, in essence, are investing in a team foundation that creates a strong base upon which you and your partner drive impressive business results together.

Attitude, Process, and Procedure Adjustment

Once you have the feedback and have honestly assessed it and internalized it, you then take the next step to do something with the feedback and adjust your "system of doing business." Your system is made up of your values, beliefs, work processes, procedures, and attitudes. Unless you are willing to break this system down and rebuild it, if necessary, then you are probably not a good candidate for engaging in a joint venture or strategic alliance.

During all of these trust-building steps, your prospective partner should also be collecting information from you, just as you are taking in information from him. And just as you are being judged on how well you accept feedback—even feedback that hurts—you should be watching how well your prospective partner hears and digests bad news and then takes positive action to make things better. If this is not happening, you may be dealing with someone who, as the old saying goes, "can dish it out but can't take it." Consider whether this is the type of individual with whom you want to partner.

If you find in your initial discussions that trust is growing and you decide to move ahead with your joint venture, keep in mind that trust building is an ongoing requirement of a good alliance. As I will discuss in greater depth later in this chapter, the Trust-building Model is a tool that can be used throughout the life of a relationship. In any partnership, people can make mistakes and erode trust; when this happens you will need to move through the model again by communicating openly about the problem, providing whatever feedback is needed, and then making any necessary adjustments to avoid similar problems in the future.

BREAKING DOWN PERCEPTIONS

The greater the trust among the parties of a joint venture, the stronger and more productive the relationship will be for all. But trust is not inherent; it must be carefully built and tended over time.

The task of building trust in a business relationship can be significantly greater when the two parties are separated by differences in race, ethnicity, or gender. As America becomes more and more diverse, so, too, do relationships in the business community.

Never before in the history of America has there been so much opportunity to engage in joint ventures and strategic alliances that cross racial, ethnic, gender, and class boundaries. According to the 2000 Census and my interpretation of this demographic shift, the American population has never been as diverse and populated with multiple critical masses of groups that are ready to leverage their knowledge and intellectual capital to change the world and revolutionize how business is done on a global level. African-Americans, who, until recently, have always been by far the largest minority group in America, now make up close to 13 percent of the population. Latino-Americans, who have grown at a rate that makes them the country's largest minority group, now make up greater than 13 percent of the overall population. With the addition of the Asian-American and Native American populations (approximately 4.5 percent of the American population) minority Americans are approaching one-third of the country's population. Not only are minority numbers increasing but minority buying power and aggregate contribution to the United States Gross Domestic Product is also increasing. In 2003, it is estimated that the combined buying power of these groups exceeded $1.5 trillion.

Because of this increased economic clout and the growing numbers of minority-owned businesses, enormous opportunities exist for groups that may have never done business together in the past to join forces to create wealth and economic opportunity for many. Increasing numbers of majority-owned and minority-owned companies are working together, as I discussed in Chapter 2. But whether it is a majority-owned business reaching out for the first time into the minority business community to try to form partnerships or businesses from two different minority communities joining together, the challenges are still great. We still have much to learn about each other before the barriers created by our differences—real or imagined—are eliminated.

To help break through these barriers, it is helpful to understand fully the perceptions held by people on both sides of the barrier you're trying to breach as you form your alliance. Guidance can be found in comprehensive surveys on intergroup relations in America done by the National Conference for Community & Justice (NCCJ [formerly the National Conference for Christians & Jews]) in 1993 and again in 2000. These studies, titled *Taking America's Pulse,* examined attitudes and experiences of Americans as related to bias, bigotry, and racism. From their results, we can learn a great deal about the challenges involved in reaching across racial, ethnic, gender, and other boundaries to build trust in business partnerships.

Here are some of the findings of the first NCCJ survey, which, among other things, looked at specific perceptions racial groups have about other groups:

- Thirty-three percent of Hispanics, 22 percent of Asian-Americans, and 12 percent of whites agreed with this statement: "Even if given a chance, blacks aren't capable of getting ahead."

- Sixty-eight percent of Asian-Americans, 50 percent of whites, and 49 percent of blacks agreed with this statement: "Hispanics tend to have larger families than they are able to support."
- Fifty-three percent of Hispanics, 42 percent of blacks, and 27 percent of whites agreed with this statement: "Asian-Americans are unscrupulous, crafty, and devious in business."
- Two-thirds of all minorities agreed that "Whites are bigoted, bossy, unwilling to share power, insensitive to other people, and have a long history of prejudice."

We can all hope these stereotypes have eased in the years since that initial study, but we know they have not been completely eradicated from the American psyche. The second *Taking America's Pulse* study revealed some cause for hope as well as areas of continued concern for those who hope to bridge racial or ethnic differences to achieve a business objective. Interesting findings in the 2000 study include:

Interracial/interethnic contact is higher now than in 1993. The report also finds that those who have greater contact with other racial and ethnic groups are more likely to rate intergroup relations as a priority and have greater feelings of closeness with other groups. This bodes well for business people who are trying to break down barriers. With greater intergroup contact comes greater understanding and a desire to improve relations overall.

Perceptions of discrimination vary among groups. Asked if they had received unfair treatment based on race or ethnicity in the 30 days prior to the survey, 41.5 percent of blacks, 29 percent of Asians, and 16 percent of Hispanics responded "yes." Only 13 percent of whites answered "yes." Understanding that discrimination is still what the report calls "a common part of the everyday lives of many Americans" is critical if you're trying to understand how the perceptions of a minority businessperson might differ from those of a white businessperson.

Among racial and ethnic groups, most say their group generally gets along with others. The lowest level of interracial/interethnic harmony is not between whites and any racial or ethnic minority but rather between minority groups. For example, when asked how their groups get along, 56 percent of blacks reported their that they generally got along with Asians; this compares to 65 percent of blacks who said they generally got along with whites. These minority-to-minority attitudes are important to bear in mind if you're a minority business owner trying to do business with a business owner from another racial or ethnic group.

Overall, 54 percent agreed that with the statement that "Until racial minorities shape up and realize they can't get a free ride, there will be little improvement in race relations in America." My main point here is that anyone who is considering a joint venture that involves breaking through any social barriers needs to be aware of the potential for differing perceptions on both sides of the table. By being aware that you may view each other through different lenses, you can be prepared to work diligently together to overcome these differences.

Please understand that I am not saying that if you are female or a member of a racial or ethnic minority, you will automatically meet with bias from your potential partner. As the survey results above indicate, although the biased views are common, they are not held by 100 percent of people. In fact, many of the misperceptions are held by very small percentages of the various groups studied. Don't go into every business deal that involves crossing racial, ethnic, or gender barriers assuming you're going to have to cope with bigoted people. However, you must approach the deal with a healthy dose of reality and be prepared to make an extra effort to "educate" your potential partner with full honesty and truth.

Also, as you try to build trusting business relationships, it is just as important to be as mindful of your own possible biases as it is to be aware of any negative stereotypes others may be applying to you. You cannot expect to be able to build real trust in a business partnership if you can't acknowledge that your dealings with potential partners may be impacted by your own racial, ethnic, class, social, or gender views. Sometimes deep-seated beliefs we aren't even conscious of interfere with our ability to deal in a trusting manner with people who are different from ourselves.

When both organizations come to joint venture negotiations with an awareness of the perceptions on both sides that might interfere with the critical step of building trust, it is more likely that the relationship can be moved forward in a positive direction. On the other hand, things can go badly off track when people try to ignore the fact that their personal biases are hindering them from being open with the other party.

ELEMENTS OF TRUST BUILDING AFTER THE DEAL IS DONE

As mentioned earlier, trust must be constantly maintained and worked on throughout the life of the relationship. Below are six components that I believe people desire in a business partner from the beginning to the end of the relationship. Consistent adherence to these behaviors goes a long way toward establishing and maintaining trust.

Attention to detail. Although we're not all perfectionists, there is a certain level of attention to detail that most people expect from a potential business partner. While we're all willing to forgive minor mistakes, none of us wants to put hard work and equity into a joint venture with a partner who is not paying attention in the same way we are. Having processes in place that make it easy to pay attention to detail will help you and your partner provide the level of attention that builds trust. Possibilities include weekly progress reports that track all the critical components of the joint venture or regularly scheduled meetings with pre-planned agendas that cover critical issues.

Honesty. Being able to depend on someone's word is perhaps the most essential component of trust. This means being open and forthright in all your dealings with your joint venture partner and not having hidden agendas. It also means not lying through omission. We all want to put the best face on things, but if a partner realizes you're failing to mention some pertinent facts because they might make you or your organization look bad, this will erode trust.

Reliability. Joint venture partners need to know they can depend on each other to deliver on promises. The same things that will doom your business even when you're not involved in a joint venture—behaviors such missing deadlines, delivering poor quality products or service, not fixing problems quickly, or not taking care of financial obligations in a timely fashion—will also lead to the quick demise of a joint venture. With so many potential partners out there, no organization is going to be willing to partner with a small business that proves itself to be undependable.

Mutual respect. The playing field between the two partners of a joint venture should be as level as possible, with each side treating the other with respect at all times. As a small business owner, the last thing you want to do is partner with an organization whose leaders act as though your organization is somehow inferior because of its small size or who, in other ways, show a lack of respect for you and the people in your company. The energy it takes to overcome such negative treatment would be far better spent in identifying potential partners who earn your trust by showing respect for what you've accomplished with your business.

Determine who will lead and who should follow. In most joint ventures, there will be a leader and a follower. This should be established from the start of the relationship based on a joint evaluation of each organization's respective strengths and weaknesses. When these roles are defined early on, it is easier to avoid misunderstandings that erode trust.

Commitment to forgive. Few organizations have the capability to provide perfect execution all the time. Thus, in any joint venture, a time eventually comes when one partner or the other makes a mistake, sometimes a big one. If you cannot commit to forgive each other, the odds of the joint venture working are slim. If you're unable to get past a mistake and are constantly holding a past error over your partner's head, the trust between the two organizations will deteriorate to the point where the relationship is unworkable. You must be able to explore together why the error occurred, put plans in place that will avoid the same or similar problems in the future, and then move forward in a positive manner.

C *a s e* S *t u d y*

DRIVING NEW ALLIANCES AT MICROSOFT

G. Winston Smith is director of Supplier Diversity at Microsoft Corporation; he joined Microsoft in 2002 after spending 22 years with AT&T. During his last three years with the telecommunications giant, he moved into Supplier Diversity after serving in a wide range of functional areas, including Network Service, Operations, Engineering, and Law and Government Affairs.

Smith's exposure to strategic alliances began after the divestiture that split AT&T from the so-called Baby Bells. In the following years, AT&T entered into a series of large alliances and mergers in search of market growth. Ultimately, nearly all of these ventures failed, leaving Smith with the opinion that strategic alliances that focus on the pursuit of market growth are problematic, while joint ventures between suppliers and vendors have a higher chance of success. At Microsoft, he has helped facilitate several vendor joint ventures that are already showing signs of success. He has also focused on helping the company build go-to-market joint ventures with minority companies. Here's the narrative of my interview with him.

Please tell me about the types of joint ventures you've participated in since joining Microsoft.

Smith: There's one involving two food services vendors, Thompson Hospitality and Compass Group USA. That's working well. Thompson, which is a minority company, and Compass, which is a majority company, have figured out what work Thompson will do and how they will interface with each other and with Microsoft. They've also figured out how to sign the contracts with the customer and how the money will flow. For us, as the customer, it feels seamless.

We just drove a deal involving Worldwide Technology and Dell whereby we buy all the peripheral equipment associated with PCs from Worldwide Technology here in the United States and for our offices outside of the country from Dell. That one is working extremely well. We really do like the Worldwide Technology folks; they just did not have the non-U.S. infrastructure to support the provisioning of that type of equipment outside of the United States.

The joint venture was implemented in a very short period of time, because Worldwide Technology had a history of working with Dell in other projects. So when it came down to a bid deal with us, they were able to bring that history to the table. They already had the product interfaces between the two of them, so working on this project with us was just an extension of an ongoing relationship they've had for years.

The joint venture between Thompson and Compass also was implemented quickly, because they had done similar joint ventures to serve other Fortune 100 companies. They were able to bring their relationships and a model to the table.

In both these cases, did the vendors bring the deal to you or did you facilitate the two companies coming together?

Smith: We helped facilitate both deals. We had just been working with Compass; Thompson was not in the picture. Thompson had a joint venture with Compass with three other Fortune 100 companies, but not with us. A couple of years ago, we began to assign diversity supplier goals to each of our category managers. At the time, the person who ran our food services procurement group told his Compass counterpart that he (the buyer) had a diversity goal and may need to re-bid the work.

The Compass executive came back and said, "I can do this if you extend the contract with us past its current expiration date." So he locked in a revenue stream for a longer period of time by simply bringing to the table a structured relationship with Thompson that he had already implemented with other companies.

For the other joint venture, we wanted to do something with the area of PC accessories in terms of more supplier diversity. When we put out the RFP, we made it clear that diversity was important to us, but even when Dell came to the table, we had to make it clear to them that this was important. That drove them to pay more attention to Worldwide Technology and implement a structure that put Worldwide first in the deal for U.S. sales and Dell first outside the U.S.

What are you hoping to do in the future at Microsoft to foster strategic alliances?

Smith: One of the areas of my focus right now is strategic alliances at the go-to-market partners stage, the revenue stage. I think that while there's a lot of work done with strategic alliances at the supplier stage among the automotive companies, defense contractors, construction companies, and so on, there's not as much being done around strategic alliances at the revenue stage.

I'm working with a company out of Nashville to be a strategic partner with Microsoft at the revenue stage. They have developed an electronic voting application using our software. When they sell their solution, Microsoft makes money, so the incentive for us to partner with them is the revenue opportunity we have. The company is not a supplier to Microsoft; it would be a revenue partner.

My sense is that there are various companies out there, minority companies, that are developing products and that are looking for the right kind of strategic partner with whom to go to market. And as they go to market, the partner makes money and the smaller company makes money.

That is not as easy as it may seem, because just as the company has to work through the intricacies of a relationship on the go-to-market side, it also needs strategic relationships on the infrastructure side and capital. So this issue of capital is a big one for these types of relationships. It's one thing if you are a supplier and have a capital issue. Then you have a receivable or a contract that you can leverage to get capital. But it's a whole different thing if you have a capital issue as a go-to-market partner, because now whoever puts money into your company has to believe you can successfully go to market.

Does Microsoft use a Tier 1, Tier 2 approach with its vendors?

Smith: It's a lot more comfortable for a Fortune 100 or Fortune 500 company to engage a large majority company, and then have that large majority company engage minority companies in a joint venture or alliance. However, I am not overly enthusiastic about that strategy. Obviously, there are places where we cannot engage a minority company directly. In those cases, I don't throw the baby out with the bathwater; I do try for a Tier 1, Tier 2 strategy, but I am constantly trying to help what might be now Tier 2 companies to become Tier 1 suppliers. In some cases, they have got to get skilled. I've been talking about this for five years; they've got to get scale and scope, where scale is breadth of operations and scope is depth of operations. To get scale and scope, smaller companies have to merge with each other, joint venture with each other, joint venture with majority companies, acquire majority companies, and do whatever it takes to morph themselves out of what they are and into what the market demands they become in order to do business with Fortune 100 companies and in global markets.

If you were advising a small or minority business, how would you advise them to turn themselves into a Tier 1 supplier?

Smith: Step one is to put together a long-term strategy for morphing the company from where it is now. First, you have to decide what you want to be when you grow up. Do you want to be a lifestyle company or do you want to be a global player? If you want to be a lifestyle company, that drives one set of strategies. If you want to become a global player and be a supplier for the Fortune 100 or Fortune 200, then that drives a different set of strategies.

If you decide you want to become a global player and have a strategy with a long-term horizon, then you want to look at the opportunities you have today and think about how to implement those opportunities. It's one thing to partner with a company to pursue an opportunity; it's another thing to partner with a company to implement the opportunity.

Creating a joint venture is kind of like the process we all go through to build a credit history. I may not need to charge $50 on my credit card, but I'm trying to build a credit history, so I go ahead and charge the $50. It's the same if you're trying to build a history with potential partners. Some of these partners are going to be companies you might acquire down the road; some of them might be companies you can joint venture with to acquire someone else; and some of them will be companies you might continue to joint venture with to give you infrastructure as you pursue other deals.

Most small business owners don't really have the time to think this through, so the other thing I advise is to surround yourself with the right kind of intellectual power. You need investment bankers. You need lawyers. You need consultants. You need people who will help you think through this strategy and help you decide how you will pull this off.

CEOs of Fortune 500 companies are constantly looking for candidates to acquire, and they have in their head the reasons why they ought to do that and how that acquisition can make their company better. The same ought to be happening with the owners of smaller businesses. If I'm in the construction business, who are other construction companies that I can acquire that would give me more infrastructure so I can have more bonding capability? And if I'm not acquiring companies, who should I be joint venturing with to go after bids and create ongoing relationships?

How would you advise a large mainstream majority company that says it wants to reach out and try to do alliances with smaller minority- and women-owned businesses?

Smith: I'd encourage them to be clear about what works in their company. We know that we much prefer alliances of majority/minority companies. We are eager to see minority- and women-owned businesses take on major operations for us, but the introduction of MWBEs into certain commodity areas is tremendously easier to implement when the firm is part of an alliance. And so, the large company that wants to reach out and do an alliance with a minority- or women-owned business may need to begin doing so initially through an alliance of such a firm and a majority company. Companies have to start somewhere. And, the objective ought not to be this year's results, but the relationship that's created and journey that the firms can travel. So, launching through an alliance is okay. Clearly, lots will need to be worked out in terms of how roles evolve over time. But so long as each party is benefiting from the relationship, there's time for roles to evolve in ways that are mutually beneficial.

5

DON'T LOSE
YOUR MOGO

"Can two walk together, except they be agreed?"
AMOS 3:3

When companies of unequal size form an alliance, too often, the smaller company goes into the deal with a built-in inferiority complex. This sense of inferiority is not necessarily based upon lack of infrastructure, limited technical ability, or even lack of past performance. Usually it is based upon nothing more than size—employee base, annual revenue, or number and size of operating plants.

Conversely, the larger company in the transaction tends to take on a superiority complex in relationship to its smaller partner. In their minds, size does matter. They conclude that because they are larger and have more employees, they must automatically be more successful than their smaller partner and, consequently, in a much better position to lead the charge. Their arrogance and myopia blinds them to the possibility that, in certain areas and scenarios, it makes better sense for the smaller firm to take charge.

I have concluded that, in such situations, the two companies have forgotten to get their "MOGO" working. No, I didn't say "mojo," a term my parents used back in the sixties and seventies to describe serendipity. I said MOGO, an acronym I created to capture the four critical elements you and a potential joint venture partner must establish as the foundation for your relationship. MOGO stands for:

- **M**ission
- **O**bjectives
- **G**oals
- **O**pportunity

Once you put these elements in place in step two in the Strategic Partnership Model, the groundwork is laid for moving forward on your joint project.

The pieces of your MOGO must be set up jointly by you and your potential partner. There can be no hidden agendas when it comes to joint venturing. All the elements must be laid out on the table and fully agreed upon. That's why building the atmosphere of trust I described in the previous chapter is so critical. From the very start of discussions about a possible joint venture, you and your would-be partner must work to clarify what you both hope to achieve by coming together.

HOW TO GET YOUR MOGO WORKING

To properly construct your MOGO requires leadership from the very top of both companies. Both leaders must be committed to the success of the venture and then support that commitment with deeds and resources. They must be systemic and holistic thinkers, being careful not to only see the discrete components of the deal but the big picture as well.

Here are the key guidelines for developing the MOGO, along with advice about how to handle some of the normal sticking points related to this process.

The MOGO's elements must be very clearly defined and thoroughly thought out. The explicitness that is required is time-consuming. This is definitely not the type of exercise you want to undertake casually. If you take a "let's write this down on the back of an envelope, shake hands, and then we're good to go" approach, you could be in big trouble down the road.

The worst thing that can happen is that you get into the joint venture project and realize that while you thought you had agreement on the MOGO, you and your partner are actually working on different missions or objectives. This is why the MOGO must be highly detailed, and nothing can be taken for granted.

For example, pay attention to definitions. Be aware that words have different meanings for different people. Make sure you know what your potential partner means when he says his company will "quickly" undertake a task. When you hear the word "quickly," you might think it means within the next month, but to the person on the other side of the table it might mean sometime this quarter. Spell out time frames and be as specific as possible about exactly what you and your potential partner are committing to do.

The MOGO must show a clear business purpose. It's not enough to like your potential partner, admire the business he or she has developed, and think it would be great to work together on something. Your two organizations must be capable of producing something together that neither company could produce on its own. Also, a market must exist for what you can produce together. If these conditions aren't met, you're both wasting your time, and there's no reason to move forward.

The business relationship must provide mutual benefits for both parties. I stressed this point in Chapter 2, and I bring it up again because it is during the development of the MOGO that you should become clear whether the relationship you're contemplating has potential benefits for both parties.

Never be so dazzled by a potential partner's size or reputation that you allow your company to be dragged into a joint venture that isn't going to provide a significant business gain for your organization. Don't lose sight of the fact that your ultimate goal is to grow your bottom line; if a joint venture doesn't move you in that direction, then there's no point to the deal.

Don't hesitate to say to a potential partner, "Upon reflection, I realize this isn't going to take my company in the direction we want to go. I'd like to work with you, but not on this particular project. It just doesn't seem right for us at this point in time." This gives your potential partner an opportunity to either change some of the deal's parameters so it becomes attractive to you or to walk away and find another company for whom the project might be right. Either way, you've done the right thing for your company by not getting bogged down in a project that would drain resources and energy without producing what you need to move forward.

Also, it can be tempting to take on a project that doesn't offer a big benefit for your company with the notion that it will lead to other projects that will produce the business growth you seek. This can be a legitimate strategy, but it's not one I recommend using in every situation. If you do adopt this strategy, be clear with your potential partner about your motivation for undertaking this initial project. He or she can confirm whether your expectations of more projects and better benefits for your company in the future are legitimate. Here again, the element of mutual trust is huge; if you have any doubt that your potential partner is not being honest about what the future might hold, it's best not to enter into the partnership. Of course, no one can predict the future, but you want to at least feel that your potential partner will make a good faith effort to fulfill any promises made about future opportunities.

Just as you need to make certain of the benefit the joint venture holds for your organization, you want to be equally concerned that specific benefits will accrue to your potential partner. If what your partner is going to get out of the deal is not substantial, you'll have to worry throughout the project about whether he's really going to be motivated to fulfill the commitment he has made. This is not something you want to have keeping you awake at night, so make sure the deal is equitable on both sides.

Agree on the target customer base, the product or service to be provided, its pricing, and, if relevant, the vendors to be used. This is another area where being clear about what specific words and terms mean to you and to your potential partner is essential. You may be tempted to define your target customer base very loosely. To use a very simple example, you might say your market is mid-sized companies. But your idea and your potential partner's idea of what qualifies as mid-sized may differ. Be explicit; talk about company size in concrete terms, such as of the number of employees or annual revenues. Then you will know you're both on the same page. Do this all across the board when you're agreeing on the target customers, the exact nature of the product, and its pricing.

If vendors will be involved in your joint venture project, decide on who those will be up front. Talk about who you both work with now and why you both like your current vendors. This will help uncover any hidden issues about what could be key relationships for helping your partnership succeed.

For example, if your partner uses a certain printer because that company is owned by his brother-in-law, but you're not impressed with that company's work, you want to discuss that issue now, not when you're at the point in the project where the printing has to be done. Both of you have to be comfortable with the choice of suppliers. The key consideration here is to consider what is best for the success and profitability of the project rather than insisting on a particular vendor for reasons that aren't related to the goals of the joint venture.

Determine the specific contribution each company will make toward the stated goals. Meeting this requirement involves looking at all the resources that will be required for the joint venture and deciding exactly where they're going to come from. Consider all aspects of the project and determine which partner will provide the capital, the people, the space, the equipment, and the infrastructure to get the job done. If some aspect of the project has to be outsourced, decide where the funding for that will come from.

Don't overlook back office or support services that will be needed for the project. Who will provide customer support, if that's a factor? Who will handle the accounting? Who will take care of getting any necessary legal work done? Try not to overlook any aspect of the project. Being clear about who is responsible for what will go a long way to avoiding conflicts as the project moves along.

While you're nailing down these project specifics, the manner in which your potential partner handles these negotiations can be very instructive as to what type of joint venture partner they will actually end up being. Are they trying to nickel and dime you on everything? Do they appear to be spendthrifts while you're very careful about your company's money? Do they seem a little too cavalier for your tastes about accounting practices?

Disagreements about money is one of the top reasons marriages fall apart, and so it is with joint ventures. Listen to your gut during these negotiations and be willing to walk away from a potential partner who doesn't appear to be a good match in terms of how they manage their finances and their financial dealings with others.

THE MISSION STATEMENT

Tons of information is available about how to develop a good mission statement, so I'm just going to review the key points. The mission statement you and your joint venture partner create should:

Be motivating. Everyone likes to know they're devoting their time to something worthwhile, so you and your partner, as well as the employees who will work on the joint venture project, should find the mission inspiring. When the joint venture hits the inevitable bumps on the road, the mission should hold everybody together with a common purpose. If the mission you and your potential partner create doesn't excite you or if it doesn't make sense within the context of the rest of your business, then you either need to revisit the mission or reconsider the joint venture. The mission should be something that will propel both businesses forward.

Stress major values that you and your partner want to honor. Many mission statements include an explanation of the values the organization espouses. A discussion around the topic of values with your potential joint venture partner can be very eye-opening. You definitely want to know that the company you are considering forming an alliance with operates out of a set of values that complement those of your organization. For example, if a commitment to innovation is a key driver of your business philosophy, you want a partner who agrees that devoting resources to being on the leading edge is important. Without agreement on values, a joint venture is almost certainly doomed.

Provide a vision and direction for the life of the joint venture. The mission should let people know where the joint venture is taking your two companies. A well-defined mission lays out the scope of the team's commitment to a type of business and its place in the market. It describes the joint venture's orientation to defending itself against intrusion or attack from competitors within the industry sector or from outside that sector. What will be different once the mission is fulfilled? What will exist that doesn't exist now if the two companies work together as a team? By showing everyone involved how things will be better as the joint venture moves forward, you will provide added incentive for them to do the hard work that is involved in partnering.

Keep in mind that there are no right or wrong mission statements. Most can be defined or expressed in terms of a core technology (e.g., nanotechnology, MEMS), industry sector, customer groups, functions performed, or goods and services offered. Here are a few examples of mission statements I have either observed or helped to develop.

The Millennium Group Mission

The Millennium Group is one of the most successful information technology services companies in the mid-Atlantic market dedicated to providing systems engineering, wireless engineering, and technology implementation services. The Millennium Group's mission is to help clients to improve their competitive positioning through the creative application of information technology to automate all essential back-office services of municipalities with a population of 500,000 or more.

The Carlyle Group's Mission

The Carlyle Group is a global provider of staffing services, staff augmentation, and outsourcing services that is dedicated to supporting companies in the biotech industry. From our operating units headquartered in Boston; Washington, D.C.; San Francisco; and Dallas; we provide our customers with the very best knowledge workers in the biotech industry, at the lowest total cost of engagement, within the shortest period of time. Our commitment to service, excellence, and expediency guides us in our mission to profitably provide the human assets necessary for the biotech industry to rapidly reach maturity.

Axion's Mission

Axion is a collaboration between three real estate development companies to find and exploit value in underutilized and undervalued urban properties. Our commitment to rebuilding the inner cities of America directs us in our mission to profitably design, engineer, and build, attractive, strategically located, and politically supported development projects in transitioning neighborhoods in urban centers that are emerging into or who are already in the midst of an urban renaissance.

GOALS AND OBJECTIVES

With the mission of the joint venture decided, it now becomes critical to build the foundation that will make the mission achievable. What makes the mission achievable is the development of well-thought-out goals and objectives. In determining what the joint venture's goals are to be, the leadership of the two companies must factor in a number of controllable factors as well as uncontrollable factors. Controllable factors are things such as the amount of capital that is raised, the specific resources and the amount of resources that each company will bring to the deal, which markets the team focuses on, and what the requirements will be for exiting the relationship. Uncontrollable factors might include:

- The condition of the economy: Are we in a recession or an expansion?
- Consumers: Are they more empowered or less empowered to make the purchasing decision the joint venture requires?
- Technology: Is the technology stable? Is it unproven? Has it achieved market acceptance yet?
- Government: What regulations are in place today that will impact the joint venture? What new regulations are being vetted that would impact the probability of success for the joint venture?
- Suppliers: Do we have a reliable and diverse supplier base that is capable of providing the materials needed for the joint venture? Are there substitutes that we should be pursuing as potential backup?

The joint venture's overall objectives are broad, measurable targets that will determine the success of the venture; these objectives can be used to compare against actual performance. Most joint ventures use a combination of market share, mind share, sales, profit, technical competence, and engineering ingenuity objectives to ultimately gauge their level of success. These objectives are often divided into short-term objectives (0–6 months), medium-term (6–18 months), and long-term (more than 18 months). The following are examples of joint ventures goals and objectives.

Goal #1

The team's ultimate success is measured by our increasing number of satisfied clients, higher client-retention rates, increased market share, and increasing efficiencies, which ultimately result in increased sales and profits:

- Objective A: Increase number of satisfied customers by 50 percent. A customer's level of satisfaction will be determined by the customer satisfaction surveys that are completed after every engagement.
- Objective B: Increase market share in target sectors by 3 percent the first year, 5 percent the second year, and 7 percent the third year. Beyond year three, maintain market share while growing revenue with the industry.
- Objective C: Maintain an EBIT at 25 percent for years 2 through 5 of the venture.

Goal #2

We will aggressively implement new and emerging technologies to advance our ability to service our clients better than anyone else:

- Objective A: Develop long-term partnership with local university to review and assess 10 new technologies each year.

Goal #3

We will make our venture fun and enjoyable because we are doing the work that we choose with the people who we like, while pursuing worthwhile and valuable business objectives:

- Objective A: Develop pool of 10 new opportunities each year and develop a team that represents both companies to determine which opportunities are pursued.
- Objective B: Define what constitutes worthwhile and valuable business objectives.

THE OPPORTUNITY

The final step in developing your joint venture's MOGO is to define the opportunity. This is critical undertaking so I have made it step three in the Strategic Partnership Model to highlight its importance. As I discussed earlier, this involves identifying who your target customer is, what types of products or services you'll be offering, what support services will be provided, and the price structure.

To develop the opportunity, you and your potential partner have to exchange enough ideas and information to assure you both that

- together you can create something of value,
- there is a market for that product or service, and
- the two organizations have the credentials and the financial wherewithal to make a creditable run at the identified target market.

In other words, you need to go deeply enough into the exercise of defining the opportunity to understand whether there truly is something that is worth pursuing for the benefit of both companies. In some cases, what the opportunity should be is immediately apparent to both companies. But this is not always the case. You both may have to devote some resources and time to finding the best answer to what your organizations can offer to what market. The offering may evolve over many discussions as you both take in new information from each other and then go back and mull it over within your organization.

If the answer you finally come up with is "Yes, together we can develop an offering and pursue an opportunity that has a solid chance of market success," then you move to the next steps of the Strategic Partnership Model, which involve evaluating both your own organization and your potential partner's organization in light of the jointly developed MOGO.

C *a s e*   S *t u d y*

CORPORATE EXPERIENCE HELPS ENTREPRENEURS MASTER THE ALLIANCE EQUATION

Jerry Sanders and Gwen Jenkins founded The Broadview Group and Broadview Staffing Services two years ago to provide temporary staffing services to the Northeast and Mid-Atlantic region. Sanders serves as CEO and president, and Jenkins serves as chief operations and marketing officer. Both Sanders and Jenkins have extensive corporate and entrepreneurial experience, a combination that enables them to understand the strengths and weaknesses of both sides when large and small companies come together as strategic partners.

From the start of their new venture, forming alliances was a part of their strategic direction. Here, they talk about their experience with joint ventures and how they are using this strategy to support the growth of their young firm.

Jenkins: When we were starting Broadview, Jerry [Sanders] and I attended a seminar given by a VC [venture capitalist]; one of the things she recommended for entrepreneurs was to find out who the big guys are in your industry—she called them the boulders of the industry—and figure out how to hug that boulder so they don't run you over. That was a message that stayed in both our heads. Partnering as a growth strategy was in our business plan, so we already knew what the VC said was important, but there's nothing like a nice story to help you keep focused.

Sanders: The VC used the analogy of boulders because a boulder is not a smooth, friendly object. There are prickly points. It's heavy, so you can get crushed. You can get cut. As an entrepreneur, you have to be able to learn to live in an environment with that prickly object. If you're trying to form an alliance with a much larger entity and that boulder is rolling down the hill, you have to be moving down the hill with it. You don't want to be going in the opposite direction, and you don't want to stand still and get crushed. So you're thinking about what's in it for the boulder. And knowing that the boulder is going to keep going down the hill, how can I take advantage of that?

What Makes Alliances Work?

Jenkins: One of the main things is a commitment to the relationship. That commitment has to be throughout the organization. Often what happens is that the CEO, the CMO, and other senior people all say, "I made a commitment to my customer through this organization that I'm going to do X amount of spending in this community," but by the time that commitment gets to the branch people who have to make it work, it's nonexistent.

It's not malicious; it's that the compensation systems reward you for bringing X amount of revenues into your base; they do not reward you for sending revenues out of your base or out of your branch to another company, albeit a minority company you're joint venturing with. So you have to have systems in place in both companies that demonstrate your commitment to the relationship.

It also takes resources on both sides of the table. We spent a considerable amount of time with a systems company in their conference room with a number of senior people in their organization hammering out a very unique joint venture agreement to take to a particular customer, and it took a lot of commitment of resources, specifically time, to hammer that out. So when we talk about commitment, this is not just saying, "This is what we're going to do." Commitment is putting the resources and time and energy into doing it on both sides.

Sanders: I think that, in addition to that commitment, the leadership of the larger partner has to understand the operational issues around how to make the relationship work. Getting to Gwen [Jenkins]'s point, the people in the trenches often are not given incentives to make it work, but if, up front, you realize that and you say, "All right, every opportunity that comes in to City A, you're going to get that," now we've eliminated the discretion down in the field about who gets what. Now we've hardwired the commitment into the organization.

Also, for those ventures that are successful, you lay out what the responsibilities are for each party up front. If you go into a venture and that is not clear, it's very easy for the large partner in the venture to take over control. If you know what your role is and you execute along those lines, you stand a better chance of having a more successful venture.

Jenkins: The flip side of this is on the entrepreneurial side. As entrepreneurs, we must be more effective at being prepared financially and operationally to handle what gets thrown our way because the customer's and the prime's reputation is on the line.

In our business, we supply people; that's a very important ingredient and therefore we have to perform. We can't say we didn't perform because we couldn't get the funding or we didn't perform because we didn't have the systems. We can't do that and expect the other company to understand and take up our slack. So this is where preparation meets opportunity. You have to be prepared on your side.

The Challenges of Uniting Small Companies

Jenkins: I think it's often the same challenges when it's a small company to small company alliance, but what can be unique is that neither company has the resources when you're trying to pull together to do something. Often it looks like a good idea until you put it on paper and you say, "Okay, what are you bringing to the table and what am I bringing to the table?" Often, what we have mirrors what the other company has; sometimes we don't have complementary strengths needed to go after an opportunity.

The other challenge I've seen came up in a previous entrepreneurial experience. We wanted to stack the deck by combining three or four entrepreneurial firms and joint-bidding a major project; we thought this would make our bid an offer the customer couldn't resist. But the biggest resistance I had was a feeling from the other entrepreneurial firms that because we were in the same business we could be in competition. They wanted to know how we could possibly form this partnership. Of the three or four firms we went to to try to put that together, only one of them said yes. And it hurt us all in the final analysis.

In talking to some companies, one of the feedbacks they've given us is that a lot of entrepreneurs who are trying to grow only want to grow to a certain level; they don't really want the big deals. They don't want to make the commitment on their side to do what it takes. So there are things on the entrepreneurial side that make some entrepreneurs poor partners, and they contribute as well to the failure of joint ventures. We are not implying by any means that it's only the larger companies' fault if things don't work.

Sanders: Many entrepreneurs don't have a lot of experience doing alliances, and because you're an entrepreneur you think in a certain way. In a joint venture, everybody has a role, and there are times when you may have to take a back seat or you may have a very different role than you would normally have.

If I've always been the boss and I'm trying to combine with someone who has always been the boss, it's very difficult for us to get past who's the boss. On the flip side, with a larger company, all the folks there are used to having a boss. So it can be a little less strenuous in getting through that hurdle.

Getting Comfortable with Corporations

Jenkins: One of the other things that I won't minimize is that Jerry and I both come from corporations; we understand the good, the bad, and the ugly of that. When you are a small entrepreneurial firm, you're making your decisions on an hour-by-hour, day-by-day, quick basis because you don't have a choice. Dealing with a corporation that says, "I'll get back to you next week on that because I have to get three signatures on approval" can be a very frustrating experience.

Entrepreneurs have to be very selective with their time. Jerry and I can work 24/7 and still not get to all the situations at the level of detail that we'd like. So we're very selective with our time, and when you're dealing with a corporation, they have their procedures, their signature processes, their approval levels of who has to see what. You're not going to change that, so you have to learn to work within it and sensitize them to your resource restraints. If you haven't been on that side, it's very frustrating, and even if you have been on that side, you still have to be very selective because you just don't have the time.

Sanders: In setting up the joint venture, there are minefields you have to navigate. For example, if you're dealing with a much larger company, you want to be sure that part of the contract terms are that you get paid quickly. You don't want to be paid late, as in they get paid in 30 days and you get paid in 40. In most cases the cash flows are there in larger corporations for you to get paid on the 30th day.

The Elephant in the Room

Jenkins: There's a softer issue that is just as critical, and that's one of trust. When you do a strategic alliance with someone who is in your industry and does what you do, you've got to trust. You can sign all the confidentiality agreements in the world, but in the end you have to trust that partner because you're sharing so much information and you're taking a very deep inside look at both companies.

A lot of entrepreneurs and a lot of big companies aren't comfortable with that because they're wondering if they're growing a competitor. That's always the elephant in the room: How much can I share? That's why long-term strategic partnerships where, for example, I work with you on some things and you work with me on some things are so much more effective and efficient. Now it's a relationship; it's not just a joint venture or alliance to go after one customer. Our best relationship is with one big partner now; we did one joint venture with them and now it looks like we're going to have three or four. All of a sudden, it's a serious relationship. They're going to know us much better than most people know us.

Partner Selection Criteria

Sanders: First and foremost, we look at what is required to meet the customer deliverable; once we understand what's required, then we're looking for a partner that complements our skill set. If it's an information technology opportunity in a geography that we're not in, we're going to look for a partner that has the resources and capabilities to make us successful in that role.

We also have some social responsibilities that we try to accomplish as we move forward, so we will typically look for a minority- or woman-owned company as a partner. That's one of our other criteria.

If it's a larger enterprise, that boulder so to speak, one criterion is whether it's a boulder that we've had a relationship with before and were comfortable dealing with them. Do we know enough people in the organization so we know we will not get crushed under the boulder's weight?

Jenkins: In large companies, we also look for sensitivity to entrepreneurs and to minority entrepreneurs, and that's evidenced in their programs and how they deal with us. We deal with HR and with procurement, and we may or may not deal with the direct operational organizations as well. It takes us a very short period of time to see that we're barking up the wrong tree because they're really not committed.

Sometimes, they've got something put down on paper and aren't committed to making it work. In that case, we aren't going to spend any time because, again, our time is just too valuable for that, as is theirs.

A mentor/protégé relationship is very important to us in our development. We can bring a lot to their table, but we want them to bring something to our table, too. We have a mentor who we can call and discuss issues. I can say, "We're looking at this opportunity, we're talking to this customer, and I'm struggling with this one area. Can you help me with it?" I have to feel you're not going to turn that around and use it on me.

So the kinds of partners we're looking for are long-term partners, whether they're majority or minority partners. We want relationships. We don't want just the relationships with the end customer. What's most important to me is a partnership because I know when I need them I can call them and when they need me they're going to call me.

Sanders: We talk a lot about strategic issues with the folks we have the strongest alliances with. If we're looking at an acquisition, they will give us feedback on what kinds of acquisitions make sense, and they'll tell us of potential opportunities for us. It truly is a mentor relationship. They are concerned about our business just as we're concerned about our business; that's how you know it's a good alliance.

6

IS YOUR
ORGANIZATION READY?

*"Individual commitment to a group effort–that is what makes a
team work, a company work, a society work, a civilization work."*
VINCE LOMBARDI

My research indicates that small
business entrepreneurs fall into four categories when it comes to
their preparedness for engaging in joint ventures and business alliances. To thoroughly evaluate their readiness and to understand
the obstacles they face in dealing with their strengths and weaknesses in this area, they need to honestly assess which group they
fall into. Here are the four different groups:

Group 1. Blood and Guts Entrepreneurs
Group 2. Brown Bomber Entrepreneurs
Group 3. Fence Walker Entrepreneurs
Group 4. Daring Dashing Dans and Dianes

Ten percent of small business entrepreneurs are Blood and
Guts Entrepreneurs, represented as Group 1 in the model in Figure 6.1.

Blood and Guts Entrepreneurs believe they can do any task
better than anyone else can. It is not that others are incapable of

FIGURE 6.1 *The Small Business Entrepreneur Joint Venture Model*

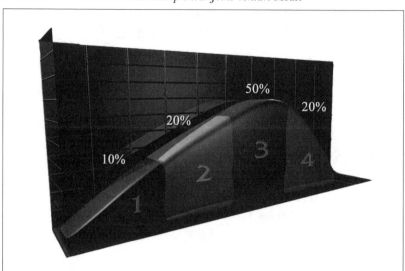

performing the task, they think, but that the work of others will be far inferior to that of themselves. Consequently, this group of small business entrepreneurs tends to do everything themselves or to micromanage the work of their staff. This approach to building one's business is limiting and will often choke the business to death. These entrepreneurs can survive, but their companies will never reach their full potential.

When it comes to their preparedness for engaging in joint ventures, they are often the last to engage and the first to disengage when the going gets tough. They follow the LIFO approach to joint ventures—Last In, First Out. Unfortunately, they often want to focus on short-term results. These folks are rugged entrepreneurs and still live by the old myth that they can make it by themselves on pure guts, determination, hard work, and a dose of good luck. Blood and Guts Entrepreneurs will only engage in joint ventures if the deal comes to them and if the deal does not interfere with their normal course of business. They are unwilling to change business processes and procedures to accommodate the possibility of engaging with and working with a business partner. They prefer to be the "Lone Ranger."

Those in the next group of the small business entrepreneur joint venture model, Group 2, are Brown Bombers Entrepreneurs. As shown in the schematic, this group constitutes approximately 20 percent of the small business universe. I named this group after one of my favorite athletes—Joe Louis, a.k.a. the Brown Bomber. I have a real affinity for Joe Louis because my dad, who at one time was a semiprofessional boxer, was one of Joe's sparring partners.

Dad often talked about how Joe was such a good man who tried to treat everyone fairly and who was kind-hearted and generous to everyone he met. Joe Louis excelled at his profession beyond anyone's imagination at that time and really perfected the art of boxing. However, my dad always reminded me that while Joe was excellent at his profession, he was naive about many other things, such as finance, business, and trustworthy relationships.

Similarly, Brown Bomber Entrepreneurs tend to be great technicians and craftsmen. These are the people who have accepted the false assumption that it is better to work "in" your business than to work "on" your business. They are content with making a "job" for themselves versus creating wealth for many. Unlike the Blood and Guts Entrepreneurs, the Brown Bombers see the inherent value in creating business alliances but are so busy working "in" their businesses that they refuse to invest the time necessary to build a successful venture with another company. People in this group are also limited in how large and how quickly they can grow their company due to their shortsightedness in the area of business alliances.

The third group, Group 3, which comprises approximately one-half of small business entrepreneurs, are the Fence Walkers. Unlike the Brown Bombers, Fence Walkers do more working "on" their businesses than working "in" their businesses. They understand the big picture of using the business as a wealth-creation engine. Consequently, they want to engage in various forms of alliances and, in fact, have even gone as far as to understand how they are done and have engaged advisors on a preliminary level.

Fence Walker Entrepreneurs have so many things competing for their limited resources that they end up completing little useful work in terms of expanding their capacity to leverage joint ventures and strategic alliances. However, as is often the case, in the short term, at least, business is going so well for them that they don't actively pursue venturing opportunities. They constantly monitor the environment for opportunities and will leap if the opportunity presents itself, but it just is not a priority for them and their management teams.

The fourth group, which comprises approximately 20 percent of the observed small business entrepreneurs, is what I affectionately call my Daring Dashing Dans and Dianes. Entrepreneurs in this group actually get it. They are what I call "Empire Builders." These guys and gals think big and dream bigger. They focus on working on the business instead of in the business, recognizing that the real benefit of owning the business is the opportunity it provides to create, sustain, and maintain a foundation of wealth on which greater business opportunities can be built.

To build their empire and to maximize their wealth creation potential, Dans and Dianes openly and joyfully embrace the concept of joint ventures and business alliances because they see this approach as an excellent strategy for accelerating the achievement of these objectives. Consequently, joint venturing is a major component of their business growth strategy, and they commit an enormous amount of corporate resources to seeking out potential alliance partners. Small business entrepreneurs in this group are very proficient with the process of structuring, building, and maintaining joint ventures. They are, in fact, so skilled in this area that other business owners seek them out for advice on these matters.

Some of you, after an honest assessment, may reluctantly put yourself in one of the first three groups discussed above. Yet others may not be sure where they fit and would rather skip the self-evaluation step of the Strategic Partnership Model. Although the groups discussed above are used to show the characteristics you might find in yourself and your company, much of what you'll do during this stage is something you should do at least annually as part of your strategic planning process. However, many business owners avoid such self-analysis *until* a compelling benefit for doing so arises, such as an enticing joint venture.

Whichever group you end up in, the objective of the self-evaluation step is to make sure your organization is capable of delivering on the MOGO you've developed with your potential partner. At the same time, you want your partner to be conducting a similar introspective analysis to make sure that company is capable of fulfilling its part of the bargain, too.

Entrepreneurs by nature are eternal optimists. We wouldn't take the chances we take as business people if we weren't positive thinkers. When we're talking with the leaders of another company about a possible joint venture, it is easy to let this confidence lead us to over-promise on what we can bring to the table. For this reason, it's essential to take a hard analytical look at your organization and its current situation before entering into any joint venture agreement.

Such analysis can be time-consuming, particularly if you haven't done any of this work lately, but I promise you'll find it worthwhile, and not just for the sake of the joint venture you're considering. The learnings you'll come away with from this self-evaluation (e.g., determining whether you are starting out as a Blood and Guts, Brown Bomber, Fence Walker, or Daring Dashing Dan Entrepreneur) will also help you plan appropriately for your company's future. It is an exercise you should go through at least once a year, especially given today's business climate in which competitive, technology, and market factors can change practically overnight with serious implications—both positive and negative—for your business.

Once you and your potential partner have both completed this self-analysis, you'll want to share the information that is pertinent to the joint venture you're considering in an incremental fashion. By incrementally feeding your potential partner bits and pieces about your company, you allow yourself time to study them and allow them a chance to reciprocate your openness and honesty.

If you're dealing with a large corporation, you will probably find that they compile much of this analysis as part of their annual strategic planning process. If, on the other hand, you're dealing with an organization that is about the same size as your own company or perhaps slightly larger, you may find they are no more accustomed to going through this process than you are. They may even be reluctant to devote time to undertaking this inward look. I encourage you to think twice about entering into a joint venture with a partner who isn't open to the idea of doing this self-evaluation or who isn't willing to share pertinent information about his or her organization with you. This could be a red flag that your potential partner lacks the business savvy to understand why this step in the Strategic Partnership Model is so essential for building trust and confidence. Or, even worse, it could mean your potential partner has something to hide about his or her organization's capabilities. Either way, it's not a good sign!

WHAT TO ANALYZE

What should you look at as part of this self-analysis? Essentially, you need to analyze every part of your business as well as the parts of the outside world that impact your ability to succeed. This means closely reviewing your company, your products, your customers, your competition, and your industry.

Here are the areas to explore:

Define your company's business purpose. Include your mission and vision and, if the vision hasn't been reviewed in a few years, make sure it still matches with where you want to take your company over the next four to five years. Depending upon your vision and mission for your firm, joint venturing may not need to be a part of your business strategy. However, I would caution you that, given the unpredictability of industries, the accelerated rate of change, a spectacular technological revolution, and emerging global economy, you should challenge any vision that does not embrace the concept of creating some form of partnerships.

Review your company's ability to build a power base within the joint venture. When assessing your company's fit for going into a joint venture, you need to quickly determine how and if the business can exit out of the alliance stronger and more powerful than when it entered. If you cannot come out better than when you went in, then what is the gain? While this outcome can't be guaranteed, there are some questions you should answer before committing:

1. Is your company relevant to the achievement of the stated MOGO? Could the MOGO be achieved without your company's input?
2. Does your company have formalized authority to make the critical decisions necessary to achieve success in the venture or does the other company have all the authority?
3. Would this opportunity allow your company to build a relationship with customers in such a way that customers understand and value the important role your company plays in helping them succeed? Would you be visible with the senior executives of the client company?
4. Are you a key component of the formal and informal networks in relating to the customer? Are you certain you always will be alerted of important developments before they become public? Will you be among the first to know when major developments occur in the customer account or even among the partnership? Obviously, you want to be a player and not a spectator.

If your answer to all of these questions is "no," you may want to reconsider this partnership. If you answered "no" to one of these questions, you need to give serious thought as to whether this deal makes sense as it is currently structured; you may want to renegotiate some of the deal's specifics to turn that "no" into a "yes."

List your product types. Do not limit this only to the products that might be involved in the joint venture—knowing the full breadth of your company's capabilities might spark ideas from your joint venture partner when you share this information. Also include products and services you would like to offer and which would meet an emerging need of either an existing or a future customer. Understand what your company lacks in bringing these new products and/or services to the market, and then look for potential partners that are strong where you are weak.

Define your pricing strategy. Companies can vary considerably when it comes to establishing a pricing strategy—a strategy that is right for one market may not be appropriate for another market. For example, technology companies that provide technical and engineering services in the public sector will find that customers in the private sector are willing to pay more for those same services, but they expect more as well.

Being clear about what your strategy is and why you think it's suitable for your market is important. Going through the exercise of putting this down on paper will help you explain your thinking to your potential partner and will serve as a basis for developing the joint venture's pricing strategy.

Define your distribution strategy. All the reasons just mentioned for why it's important to commit your pricing strategy to paper hold true for your distribution strategy. However, keep in mind that the methods and strategies of distribution in the world are changing at the speed of light. As the customer consumes more and more of the value chain, the entrepreneur must constantly seek new and novel ways to contribute to the remaining value chain. I am often asked which aspect of a joint venture relationship holds the most value. In other words, what is the most valuable asset to bring to the table? While owning the customer relationship always comes first on my list, owning the distribution channels is often a close second.

List your personnel, their positions, and skills sets. Depending on the size of your organization, you don't have to include everybody, but make sure the key players who will be involved with leading the joint venture effort are part of this list. Preparing this list will help you identify any holes in your organization in terms of skills that need to be filled for you to hold up your end of the joint venture.

Getting **Y**our **S**taff **R**eady for **J**oint **V**enture **S**uccess

When you have built your list and identified the key personnel, take these steps to prepare them for the joint venture:

- Communicate the importance of the joint venture and what it means for the company's future well-being and success.
- Explain to your personnel what their roles will be in the joint venture.
- Create a forum where people can ask questions about the joint venture so you can learn of any concerns they have that might impact the partnership's outcome.
- Make sure your people are qualified and well trained and that advanced training is made available to them on a regular basis.
- Provide an opportunity for the staff to grow and take risks. Encourage them to take risks and exercise good judgment, but be there to catch them if they fall. It is okay to fall every now and then; just make sure that it is not fatal.

List and assess your production site capabilities. If the joint venture will involve the actual production of a physical product, this is obviously a critical step. But even if the joint venture involves a non-tangible offering, there may still be important physical capacities to define. For example, if you and your joint venture partner are going to offer seminars and you happen to have a conference room complete with audio/video equipment and theater-style seating for 50 people, this should be defined as an asset to the joint venture.

Don't just assume that you already have all of this information in your head; consult with your staff, who may have some surprises for you. For instance, a client who was considering a joint venture with an Italian company completely underestimated the amount of actual production capabilities his company had. It wasn't until the president of the Italian company came to visit the U.S. site that our client's plant engineer notified him of the expanded plant capacity, which was due to new manufacturing technology that a local university had helped them implement.

Define your marketing strategy. Look at the tools and techniques you've used successfully to market your current products or services. Use this as a base for a discussion with your potential partner on how the two of you will market your new initiative. Also, this part of the exercise will help you identify any weaknesses you have with regard to marketing. Depending on how much of the responsibility for marketing the joint venture that your organization will be taking on, you might find places where you need to improve your company's capabilities or defer to your potential partner if they have more expertise in this critical area.

LOOKING OUTWARD

Once you've done a thorough review of the internal workings of your organization, you need to turn your eyes outward. What new products are emerging in your market with the potential to replace what you are currently selling? Are there services that your customer might like to have and is willing to pay for, but which you currently don't provide? It's important to survey the competitive landscape since, even if everything inside your organization and that of your potential partner is in great shape, there may be something happening externally that could impact your joint venture.

For this industry analysis, look at:

New players. Who has entered the industry since the last time you did an industry review? How do their market offerings compare with yours? What has their impact been on your business, if any? A visit to competitors' Web sites can be very helpful in gathering data for this analysis. Don't overlook press releases posted there that might give clues to their future plans.

Market size. What is the overall size of the market you operate in? Are new customers entering the market or is the market shrinking? Are there underserved demographic, geographic, or niche segments in the market that you could exploit?

Dollar volume. Is the value of the entire market growing or declining? Are you in a market where the product or service is in danger of becoming "commoditized," which will lead to falling prices? If so, this presents a whole new set of challenges, particularly in regard to marketing, that you and your potential joint venture partner will need to discuss.

Number of players. How many competitors do you have? Look beyond just the companies that sell the same product or service as you do to businesses that offer a possible alternative solution to the problem you solve for your customers. Anyone who is in competition for the same dollar as you are can legitimately be called a competitor.

International influences. Are there ways in which globalization currently impacts your business that are likely to change? Are there any emerging global economic factors that might alter how you do business in the coming years?

Major change factors. Analyze any trends that are changing how the people in your market look upon your product or service. For instance, if you're in the consumer market, is the demographic population that uses your product growing or declining? If you're in the business-to-business market, what trends are impacting the businesses you sell to that might affect their ability or desire to continue purchasing your product?

This is also the place where trends in technology need to be considered. Is a technology emerging that will make your product obsolete or lower your costs of production? This is not the place for wishful thinking. Think of the buggy whip manufacturers who no doubt spent a lot of time in the early 20th century hoping the automobile wouldn't really catch on. Be hard-nosed and realistic about your market and its technology trends to avoid a fate similar to those of the buggy whip makers.

Historical information. What have the major trends in your industry been over the past decade? How easy or difficult has it been for you to adjust your business to align with past trends? While the past is no guarantee of the future, knowing that your company has been agile enough to deal effectively with past industry changes can be reassuring not just to you but to a prospective partner.

Industry age. Is your industry reaching its maturity or is it still in its young, highly volatile formative years? Both of these situations present their own unique challenges that need to be considered.

Your market share. Is your market share going up, going down, or remaining stable? If it's moving in one direction or the other, why is that occurring? What are you doing right that you need to keep doing if your market share is growing? If it's falling, what do you need to correct? What do you want your market share to be in the future and what is your plan for achieving that?

Regulatory influences. What regulatory changes are being discussed at the national and state level that could impact your business? Even if you're in an industry that isn't subject to heavy regulation, developments that affect all businesses, such as the telemarketing "do not call" list enacted in 2003, can make it necessary to change some aspect of how you do business. Being aware of potential new regulations is essential—the last thing you want to do is invest time and money in a joint venture that is going to be blown out of the water by a new regulation.

THE SWOT EXERCISE

By this point, you've accumulated a lot of information on your company and your industry. What you do next is critical to determining whether you come away from this self-analysis with any real learnings that will help your company, in general, and the joint venture, in particular, move forward. You are now armed with all the information you need to complete a SWOT analysis of your organization. This is a widely used business analysis tool that helps companies identify their **S**trengths, **W**eaknesses, **O**pportunities and **T**hreats. Strengths and weaknesses are internal factors; opportunities and threats are external factors.

A strength could be:

- Your company's marketing and sales expertise
- A new, patent-protected product
- The location of your business
- Your company's strong relationships with distributors
- Your company's relationship with the customer
- Your company's engineering and manufacturing skills and experience
- Your company's patents and intellectual property
- The debt-free financial position of your company

A weakness could be:

- An inferior sales force
- Poor leadership
- A reputation for poor customer service
- Heavy debt
- Abnormally high product costs
- An inability to think outside the box

An opportunity could be:

- A new market niche that you can serve and that hasn't been identified by anyone else
- A potential joint venture or alliance
- The failure of a major competitor

A threat could be:

- An emerging technology that makes your product obsolete
- A new government regulation that will significantly increase your cost of doing business
- A new competitor with superior marketing and sales expertise
- Cheaper products in your field from an overseas competitor.

A SWOT analysis can be very subjective; the answers two people put in the same fields of the analysis can vary greatly. This is why it's a good idea to do this as a group exercise among your leadership team so that all viewpoints get a thorough airing, and so that consensus can be achieved on the end product. Here are some simple rules for using SWOT:

1. Be realistic about the strengths and weaknesses of your business. There's no use going through this exercise unless

you are willing to take off your rose-colored glasses and see the organization as it really is. The discussions your team has had in the process of compiling all the information in the self-analysis and industry analysis should have prepared you to put the hard facts on the table.

2. Your SWOT analysis should distinguish between the present and the future. Prepare one analysis that looks at today's facts and one that is forward-looking. This exercise is a roadmap of what needs to change to get you to the future you foresee for your business.

3. Analyze issues in relation to your competitors. Are you better or worse at something than your competitors?

4. Understand that some strengths can also be weaknesses in other contexts. For example, your location might be great in terms of how it enables you to serve your current market; however, if your long-term aim is to serve a much broader geographic area, your location may be a weakness in that context.

5. Keep your SWOT analysis brief. Avoid over-thinking the whole thing. You want an end product that lets you quickly understand where the company is now and where it can go. This is not the place for crafting beautiful sentences. Use bullet points.

By now, you're probably exhausted by the notion of going through this process of self-analysis. It can, in fact, be time-consuming. But I hope you have also realized how valuable the learnings are that come out of such an undertaking. Not only is it an effort that is well worth making in the context of preparing for a potential joint venture, but it is also a motivating exercise for moving your business forward. By defining what's right about your company, what needs to be improved, what opportunities are being presented to you by the outside world, and what dangers are lurking around the corner, you will be better armed for leading your business every day.

TWO PERSPECTIVES ON ALLIANCES FROM FREDDIE MAC

Since its founding in 1970, Freddie Mac has financed one out of every six homes in America. Freddie Mac was chartered by Congress to keep money flowing to mortgage lenders in support of homeownership and rental housing. As a stockholder-owned institution, Freddie Mac supplies lenders with the money to make mortgages, and then packages the mortgages into marketable securities. Through its activities, Freddie Mac sustains a stable mortgage credit system and reduces the mortgage rates paid by homebuyers.

As manager of Supplier Diversity at Freddie Mac, Jay Inouye's role is to make sure opportunities and doors open for minority- and women-owned businesses wanting to do business with Freddie Mac. Craig Nickerson, vice president of Community Development Lending, is responsible for the design and implementation of Freddie Mac's single-family affordable housing public-private lending initiatives. Through their vast experience with Freddie Mac, both Nickerson and Inouye have invaluable insight into the topic of strategic partnerships.

Building Community Alliances

Nickerson: When we are working to reach underserved segments of the homeownership market, especially minority families, low and moderate income households, Freddie Mac engages in broad-based alliances. These alliances support our affordable housing mission. It's important that we look toward building alliances that make sense for the geography and the population we're targeting, so that means we look toward national, regional, and most often local relationship-building to accomplish our goals. Over the last three years, I estimate we've built more than 100 strategic homeownership lending alliances across the country.

At Freddie Mac, we look to find the right organizations and companies to be part of an ongoing and long-term solution. We look for sustainable solutions, not just a "quick fix" that results in a nice press event. In the beginning of this collaborative process, we often seek out partners who are locally based non-profit and for-profit entities. One way to look at it is: the sum can be greater than the individual parts; working together, we can achieve more than we can as individual organizations. This is how we aspire to continue building our strategic alliances.

Let's look at one example, a major property renovation program, located in a predominantly African-American urban neighborhood. The first question we ask is, "What organizations do we reach out to?" We may reach out to the faith-based community, to a neighborhood housing center, to the city government, and maybe to a builder or two. Next, we ask, "What loan products and outreach approaches seem appropriate?" Once we identify what will work, we forge an alliance to achieve a success that otherwise couldn't be achieved had we tried to meet the goal on our own.

I'd say two out of every three of these special alliances are successful, but in reality there really are no failures. We view our strategic alliance program as a series of pilot efforts, almost like a form of R&D. When you are consciously going out there to try to make something happen, experimenting with new ideas, new mortgage approaches, new outreach and education initiatives, you're going to have wins and losses. By our count, we believe between 60 to 70 percent of the time we are either somewhat successful or very successful, and the other third of the time we learn how to do it better the next time. Typically, our objectives are defined as increasing mortgage opportunities for a segment of the underserved population in America or reinvigorating a geographic neighborhood. If we accomplish these things, we put them in the win column.

Part of the premise behind our alliances is that while Freddie Mac is a big organization that has a significant reach throughout the country, and has resources and a broader perspective than organizations at the local level, we need different eyes and ears within the community to be effective. We are pragmatic enough to realize that there are smaller firms and grassroots organizations at the local level that are much more in touch with the community.

Secondly, what we've learned is that the 20th-century approaches that we and our lenders may have used successfully in the past don't necessarily bode well for the needs of the 21st-century family. Two out of every three new household formations in America over the next ten years will be minority families. If these new households are going to become the first-time homebuyers of the future, we can't rely on the way we used to do things in the past. Freddie Mac could claim, "We get it. We understand it. We're totally in culture with the new buyer," but we'd be fooling ourselves. Corporate arrogance does not result in market excellence. We need a grassroots approach and people with unique technical expertise, partners who understand intrinsically the needs of the minority community.

A good strategic alliance is typically a result of picking the right partners. Clearly, a one-size-fits-all mindset does not work. We look for organizations that complement one another and that share a common vision. Successful partners are also those who listen before they talk. Too often we find organizations wanting to prove their worth; they jump in quickly but don't really take the time to listen and to understand local needs. Over-zealous business candidates come up with what they believe to be a solution before asking fundamental questions, such as what are your needs, what's holding you back, and what are your problems.

The most important ingredient for a successful alliance is building a true team, a team that offers a broad base of skills and resources and develops a cohesive game plan. It's like pieces of a puzzle. When the puzzle pieces are scattered on the table, they have no meaning. Connected together, each piece in its place, you see a clear picture.

Other issues we have to deal with when working with these alliances are more related to the size of the companies and how long they've been in business. New businesses will always undergo growing pains. They'll make mistakes. They'll sometimes over-promise and under-deliver because they're anxious to build a client base. We realize that even though you're a competent organization, you may take on more than you can actually accomplish. Every emerging firm faces these issues and, until they are successfully addressed, it will be difficult to pursue strategic partnerships.

We look for organizations that are motivated by results, responsive to the person or the organization they're working with, and dedicated to meeting the needs of underserved households who deserve a chance at owning a home of their own.

From the Procurement Side

Inouye: As any large business, at Freddie Mac, we look for companies that have scalability. We're looking for vendor alliances with a substantial-sized team, standardization of processes, cost focus, and product uniformity. Smaller businesses typically do not have the resources to deliver some of the things we want them to deliver, and so to meet our needs, we encourage these smaller companies to enter into teaming arrangements.

Through my association with minority-owned business organizations and other corporations, I have seen about 20 alliances/joint ventures. I estimate that about 20 percent have been successful or effective. I believe the main reason more of these alliances aren't successful is that many of these partners get together thinking they're a good match. In reality, however, they discover they are not.

The small business alliances that have had success work, in part, because they bring more customization to the table as opposed to larger businesses that don't typically have the same type of flexibility. In minority- and women-owned businesses, we have seen a high level of responsiveness. These businesses demonstrate that they know what the customer wants and how to respond in a customer-focused, unique solutions–oriented manner.

While it can be discouraging to be turned away, my belief is that many smaller firms target companies that are simply too large for them to do business with. The best results we see come from targeting mid-sized corporations who have less bureaucracy, more room for flexibility, and may be quicker to respond.

Another challenge small, minority- and woman-owned companies face when attempting to forge a strategic alliance is that all parties and personalities involved are typically dynamic and controlling. This is not a bad characteristic; it's the characteristic of a leader, but when you bring two entrepreneurial minds together, oftentimes you experience management struggles. Different visions, different strategies, and different certainties about how things should run, even with the same group objective, can lead to a breakdown. The issue of control will always be present. How to resolve that is the $64 million question. I think it takes good legal advice, and it's worth the investment. The lawyers are the ones who shepherd you through the realities of what it all takes to make the partnership successful.

Companies of all sizes that want to meet potential alliance partners should get involved in organizations where they'll be exposed to the business community. For example, we are very strong participants in the Virginia Minority Supplier Development Council. We provide office space to them in our building, and since they are based in Richmond, Virginia, we are able to provide space for a director and a part-time person to service the Northern Virginia area. The office organizes presentations from government bureaus, like Homeland Security, and from corporations, and it brings people together so they can see one another initially.

There are plenty of venues that both large and small companies can take advantage of to expand their networks. It doesn't necessarily always have to be procurement-focused. You can meet through volunteer programs or participate in charity events where you will be working side-by-side with people who are potential networks for you.

When I view a partnership or an alliance, it's not about getting one contract; it's about developing a long-term committed relationship. You are creating a partnership, so there is value to both parties going forward. The first step in that is to simply get out and meet people.

7

KNOWING YOUR
PARTNER

"Getting to know you, getting to know all about you.
Getting to like you, getting to hope you like me.
Getting to know you, putting it my way, But nicely,
You are precisely, My cup of tea."
OSCAR HAMMERSTEIN, CHORUS OF *GETTING TO KNOW YOU*

What do you do when a potential joint venture comes your way but you don't really know the other party? What type of due diligence do you engage in? How do you know when it is right and when it is wrong? Although there are no absolute answers to these questions, I have seen enough anecdotal evidence over the years that can provide you with some guiding principles on how to handle such situations through the further exploration of my Strategic Partnership Model.

As is true with the self-analysis work discussed in the last chapter, the next step of the Strategic Partnership Model is one that entrepreneurs often take too lightly before embarking on a joint venture. This is the "Know Your Partner" step, in which you closely examine your potential partner so you can make a well-informed decision about whether this is, indeed, a company you want to do business with.

WHY DO WE TRY TO AVOID THIS STEP?

Why do entrepreneurs shy away from doing the due diligence examination of their prospective partners that is so crucial to making a sound judgment? Obviously, doing a thorough job with this step is time-consuming, and that may be part of the reason why people tend to skip it. Not only is it time-consuming, but it also opens up other channels of risk. What if you offend the other person? What if he decides to partner with someone else before you can complete this step? What if you divulge too much information about yourself and your company and he turns around and uses it against you in some other venue? These are all reasonable concerns and could sometimes persuade the entrepreneur not to engage in this analysis.

But before you run away from doing your due diligence, consider that your potential partner should be examining your company as well. He should, therefore, understand your motivation for asking questions. Consider that anyone who is bothered by your need for due diligence may have something to hide!

However, I think the bigger reason some entrepreneurs don't like this step of the process is that, as I mentioned in the last chapter, entrepreneurs are optimists by nature. As such, we tend to get excited about a new business opportunity and just assume we can make it work. If we didn't have this inherent belief, we might not be in business for ourselves to begin with—it takes a high degree of optimism to believe you can beat the dauntingly high odds against business success.

So, when faced with an intriguing business opportunity that involves forming a strategic partnership, we tend to be optimistic about the person on the other side of the table. If our potential partner *appears* to be a successful businessperson, we would prefer to just get on with the deal rather than take time to do the digging required to learn if our first impression is correct.

If I could, I would erect a big stop sign in your office to remind you to *never* skip this step. If you do find yourself tempted to move forward with a partnership before truly getting to know your potential partner, take a minute to think about what you're risking. You've worked hard to build your business, its client base, and its reputation. Even if you're considering only a loosely coupled joint venture, some portion of what you've created for yourself and your company will be at risk if your partner proves to be unable or unwilling to deliver as promised. And if the proposed joint venture is a moderately coupled or closely coupled partnership, you're putting a great deal of what you've built on the line. Make it a rule to not proceed without gaining a thorough knowledge of your potential partner; this will protect you from unpleasant surprises as the joint venture moves forward and will minimize your risk.

ASSESSING A POTENTIAL PARTNER'S LLIFT

Determining if a business is a good match for your organization first requires conducting a review of the characteristics of the potential partner.

Remember that you only want to engage with firms that you think have a strong possibility of being a long-term partner. Why waste the investment in time, talent, and resources that is necessary to nurture relationships with a company that you know will not be in for the long haul? Your resources are too limited to waste on such an unproductive exercise.

By identifying a potential partner's characteristics, you can place him and his company in a personality category. In the previous chapter on self-examination, I suggested four personality categories that you might fit into as an entrepreneur. If you're partnering with a small firm, your potential partner might fit into one of these, too. Later in this chapter, I will suggest a similar set of personalities for potential partners that fall into the large company category.

Faced with a possible joint venture, the first step is to determine if your potential partner is a small or a large business. A rule of thumb I use is that if a company has less than 250 employees and sales less than $50 million per year, it is a small business. Under small business, I also include companies that are defined as micro-enterprises: these tend to be businesses that employ five or less people and whose capital requirements for operating the business tend to be no more than $25,000.

Conversely, a large company is defined as a company that has 250 employees or more and annual sales exceeding $50 million. Now, I am aware of the fact that the Small Business Administration defines small business differently than I do. Keep in mind that, for this exercise, I am grouping the businesses based upon characteristics and not just size. Also, there are medium-sized companies to consider in an analysis such as this, but to keep the model simple, I usually categorize the potential partner company as either large (Tier 1) or small (Tier 2).

Once you have determined whether the candidate is small or large, the next step is to define the criteria by which you will determine the candidate's most appropriate personality bucket. Based upon my research, the following criteria are offered for your consideration:

- Likeability
- Longevity
- Interest or Incentive
- Financial Muscle and Commitment
- Timeline

I call this the LLIFT model. Let's look at each of these factors closely:

Likeability

The likeability factor is very important. No matter how hard you try, it is almost impossible to work with someone you don't like. Yes, you can go through the motions of doing business together, but you will dread the experience, seek ways to minimize contact, become more and more reluctant to take any risk with the company, and most certainly will not be at your very best.

One way to determine where you are on the likeability scale is to observe how much you care about the people representing the company and the company itself. Do you go out of your way to help them when they are in need? Do you like spending time with them either at work or outside of the office? Are you comfortable sharing personal information with them? Do you commit to returning their phone calls in a very timely fashion? These are all some things to consider when determining likeability. But however you assess this criteria, be very clear on this point; business alliances where the two partners do not like one another tend not to work. There are exceptions where a relationship like this can work from a business perspective, but I guarantee you that the deal will never truly reach its full potential for reaping mutual benefits.

The other reality is that making the venture work will require that you spend an enormous amount of time together. What drudgery it will be if the two of you can't stand one another. You may not have to love your partners, but you most certainly should like them.

In judging a potential partner's likeability, you also want to do something that I call "meeting the family." This is meant literally, in that you should meet the spouse or significant other of the person with whom you're considering partnering. It's also meant figuratively, in that you should meet the individual's business family, including managers who will be instrumental in making the joint venture a success, vendors, and major customers. If there are investors in the company, meet them too.

If you truly want to get to know someone and her business, you can't just leave it at the level where the two of you are interacting. You have to reach beyond that individual and reach into her world. You may want to set up a chart on which you write down the positive and negative impressions you gain during this meeting-the-family phase.

Again, this can be time-consuming, but never doubt its value. As we all know, people can be very good at maintaining a false front. They can look good on paper and they can say all the right things. But if you peel back the layers of the onion by talking with others and by seeing how your potential partner interacts with those who know him well and who have a history with him, you may see things you didn't see before.

Getting to know other people at your potential partner's business may also uncover problems. In many small businesses, there is a steep dropoff between the leader and the rest of the organization in terms of brainpower, skills, and experience. Perhaps the middle managers haven't bought into the idea of the joint venture. Or perhaps they are not really good at their jobs. You need to know this because the fate of the joint venture could rest in the hands of such people. If, in your view, the people in your potential partner's organization don't measure up, this may impact how you structure the relationship or deter you from entering into the relationship altogether.

Longevity

The longevity factor determines what the probability is that the two companies will enter into another joint venture or partnership together. As previously mentioned, you should never begin the process of building a joint venture or alliance with a company if you know beforehand that you would not want to work with this company over the long haul.

You always want to invest in the long-term, never the short-term. Make your investment count by building a relationship with a partner you could see yourself doing multiple deals with and with someone who can help you grow, build your internal competencies, and maximize your market coverage.

Another factor to look at regarding the longevity potential of a prospective partner is the firm's history with regard to partnering. This is definitely an area you'll want to explore in a conversation with your potential partner. If you have partnered before, come to this discussion armed with information on your own history to encourage an exchange of pertinent information.

If things went poorly for your potential partner in a previous joint venture, don't assume that the explanation being given to you is an objective look at the reasons the partnership fell apart. There are two sides to every story, and you absolutely want to know the other side of this one. You need to know if the former partner has a dramatically different view of what happened. Once you hear from both sides, it's up to you to decide which explanation sounds most probable. Usually, the reality of the situation will be somewhere in the middle of the two accounts.

Interest or Incentive

Joint ventures work best when the interests of both partners are well aligned. If your potential partner's incentive for moving the work forward isn't similar in size to your own, this mismatch can lead to trouble down the road as differing priorities produce bottlenecks or similar problems.

Have a conversation with your potential partner in which you both answer the question, "What's in it for me?" Your answers should show that you each have a level of motivation significant enough to assure that the commitments involved on both sides of the deal will be met.

If the self-interest of a potential partner is far weaker than your own, consider finding another company whose motivation more closely mirrors your own. This will help you avoid frustrating scenarios in which you can't move a project forward because your partner's plate is full of things that are more vital to his company.

An interesting exercise that can help uncover discrepancies between your motivation and that of the other company is to have each of you indicate where you think the strategic partnership fits on the Joint Venture Continuum (see Chapter 1). If this uncovers a difference of opinion, this can spur a revealing discussion that may get to the heart of the issue of interest and incentive for doing the deal.

Another important source of information on your potential partner is the company's mission statement. Does this mission make sense in view of the mission you're developing together for the joint venture? In other words, is it clear how the joint venture's mission statement will help further the aims of your potential partner's mission statement? If the connection between the two is vague, you may want to ask more questions about your would-be partner's motivation.

As discussed in Chapter 6, you'll also want to share with your possible partner at least some of the information you've developed during your self-analysis exercise. Obviously, the depth you go to in sharing this information will vary according to the type of joint venture being considered. If it's going to be a loosely coupled relationship, there may be no need for either of you to share in-depth information other than about the specific aspect of your companies that will be directly involved.

If, on the other hand, you are considering a tightly coupled relationship, I would encourage you to share every pertinent bit of information you have, including your respective SWOT analyses. If you're going to be that closely linked with another organization, you both need to know as much as possible before signing on the dotted line.

Financial Muscle and Commitment

How is this organization's fiscal health? Does it have the financial wherewithal to deliver what it's promising for the proposed joint venture? Does its credit history match well with that of your own company? If you pride yourself on paying vendors promptly, you might hesitate to partner with a slow payer since that might damage your company's vendor relationships. Or, knowing this, you might suggest that your organization take charge of the joint venture's vendor payments.

Comprehensive credit reports on small businesses can be purchased from D&B (formerly Dun & Bradstreet) at http://smallbusiness.dnb.com. If your potential partner is a public company, get an annual report and carefully review the financial statements. Check their Web site for press releases on their latest quarterly earnings reports. As we've seen all too often, even giant corporations can go bankrupt, so just because a large company is wooing you doesn't mean you can skip checking on their financial well-being.

Another way to learn useful information about a company's fiscal health is to ask around within the industry. For example, talk to vendors you share; ask if there have been any problems with getting paid on time. If you have good relationships with these vendors, they will usually be willing to share such information with you if you tell them why you're asking. Make it clear that you're not seeking gossip; you have a good business reason for wanting to know. You might also consider asking your potential partner for some financial references. Provide your own references, too, to make him feel more comfortable about giving out such information.

The point is to know in advance what degree of risk you're taking so you can make an informed decision based on your own degree of risk tolerance.

The other thing you want to look at regarding finances is the level of commitment your potential partner is making to the proposed strategic partnership. Is he expecting you to put in a disproportionate share of the needed capital? Does he have an unrealistic viewpoint of what it will take financially to make the joint venture work? Disparities between what the two of you believe is required financially to make the joint venture successful are red flags that indicate money issues might make this deal fall apart sooner or later. It is far better to know this before making the deal than discovering it once you're in it.

Timeline

The timeline for a joint venture project needs to be discussed before you enter the deal. Both parties need to be comfortable with the project's proposed timeline. If your partner tries to rush you into a project that you're not ready for or to slow you down when you really need to move forward for the sake of your business, this company may not be a good fit for you. Such disparity of thinking about the timeline may indicate that the incentive for the joint venture is not balanced between you and your potential partner.

Please note that your criteria by which you evaluate your potential partner may differ from the ones I've suggested. I would encourage you to adapt the criteria to meet your specific situation and needs.

PLACING YOUR PARTNER IN A BUCKET

At this point, if you have determined that your potential partner is a small business and you have defined the criteria for judging the company's suitability as a partner, you are ready to deposit the candidates into their respective personality categories. If you start with the personalities I have defined in the previous chapter for small business partners, the four groups your candidates might fall into are:

Group 1. Blood and Guts
Group 2. Brown Bombers
Group 3. Fence Walkers
Group 4. Daring Dashing Dans and Dianes

FIGURE 7.1 *Joint Ventures: T1 Companies*

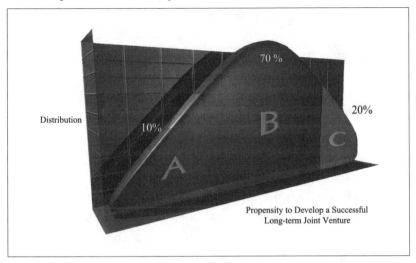

These categories were covered in the previous chapter, so I will focus here on the personality groups to consider for large companies. Based on my research, large companies fall into one of three groups as shown in the schematic in Figure 7.1.

Doomers (Group A). Some large companies fall into the well-worn trap of believing the hype about themselves. Typically they will have already enjoyed a certain level of success on their own and don't see why their position should or would change. Consequently, these people see no inherent value in reaching out to enter into joint ventures. Since they view themselves as so successful already, they are not open to the possibility of new arrangements.

If such a Tier 1 company is receiving pressure from a customer to "share" with Tier 2 firms, they will obfuscate the situation and delay it as long as possible. Even if they ultimately do engage in an alliance, they are extremely difficult to work with.

Reluctant Warriors (Group B). While Reluctant Warriors offer some level of resistance to the idea of joint venturing, they are open to the possibility, but the arrangement has to be on their terms. The reason they don't do more joint venturing is because they are so very busy. If an opportunity comes to them neatly packaged so they don't have to work too hard to make it work, they are game. They tend to show no preference to either doing an alliance or not doing it. However, if they do engage, at the first sign of difficulty or trouble, they throw in the towel. Too often these businesspeople fail to see the big picture benefit of forming strategic business alliances.

Blue Skyers (Group C). These businesspeople get it. You don't have to sell them on the idea because they are already sold! They come to a potential engagement already focused, energized, motivated, and committed to making it work. Similar to the Daring Dashing Dans and Dianes, these entrepreneurs recognize that the only way they will achieve their mission and exceed their business objectives is through the aggressive pursuit of alliances. Consequently, joint venturing is a major thread in the meshwork of their strategic business process.

The leaders of these companies tend to be outgoing, charismatic, insightful, and well positioned in their industry. They are risk-takers, but they are prudent. Once they have engaged in a joint venture, they remain engaged even if the arrangement becomes more difficult to manage. These people look for common ground, commit to building a consensus, and are anxious to use the existing business relationship as a launching pad to enter into even more joint ventures with other companies. Blue Skyers believe that business alliances are true business ecosystems that will grow, shrink, and adjust to the constantly changing external and internal environments.

You may assume from my description of these three groups that unless your potential Tier 1 partner is a Blue Skyer, there is no chance of ever completing a successful joint venture with the company. Not so! The reality is that a company in any one of these groups is a good candidate for a joint venture. The only difference is that once you know what group the company leader falls in, the strategy you use to engage, structure the deal, and ultimately close and maintain the deal changes accordingly.

"Some Tier 1 companies may be reluctant to let go of the technology," T. Williams of Toyota told me. "So if you're trying to partner with a company that exhibits this characteristic, you need to consider how to best leverage and optimize your own resources."

The nice thing about life and business is that everything changes. The economy changes, the climate changes, businesses change, and yes, even people change. For example, your potential partner may start out as a Doomer, but you decide he has the exact skills and resources to meet the needs of the customer. You commit yourself and your resources to structuring and managing the venture to minimize your risks and, at the same time, manage around that partner's idiosyncrasies.

Once the alliance is proven to be successful and your partner begins to see the tangible benefits of forming this strategic alliance, you may notice a shift in the company's perspective and an increase in their propensity to do another joint venture with you. Specifically, they will begin to transition to either a Reluctant Warrior or even a Blue Skyer. Usually the shift is incremental, and rarely does a Tier 1 partner jump directly from a Doomer to a Blue Skyer.

IN THE END, FOLLOW YOUR INTUITION

After gathering as much business information as possible on your potential partner, and after getting to know him or her as well as possible, your final decision may well come down to a gut feeling.

To uncover what your intuition is telling you about your potential partner and his organization, here are some questions to consider:

- Does the quality and honestly of this individual and his organization impress you?
- Would you feel proud introducing this person as your business partner?
- Do you feel you can be totally open with her, or do you feel you should be guarded about what information you share?
- Is this someone you want to spend a lot of time with?
- Would you be proud to own the business your potential partner has built?
- How comfortable would you feel knowing that at least a part of your company's future and well-being are in the hands of this person?
- Does this person show the leadership skills you believe are essential to business success?
- Is there anything about this person that bugs you? Even if just a tiny nagging feeling, try to identify its source. This can be a very revealing exercise, since that fleeting irritation may be your intuition trying to break through your natural optimism with some bad news about your potential partner.

Through the answers to these and similar questions you develop on your own, you should be able to get to the heart of the issue of whether this is the right partner for you and your business.

C a s e   S t u d y

OBSERVATIONS ON ALLIANCE SUCCESS FACTORS FROM NMSDC'S LEADER

Harriet Michel is no stranger to the issues and challenges that face small businesses in general and minority businesses in particular. She lives, breathes, and eats minority business development. As president of the National Minority Supplier Development Council Inc. (NMSDC), which was chartered in 1972, she and her staff have built an extremely successful organization whose primary objective is to provide a direct link between corporate America and minority-owned businesses.

Part of NMSDC's success as an advocate for the advancement of minority businesses is attributable to its adroitness at mastering the concepts of building effective joint ventures and business alliances as a part of its own internal business strategy. By facilitating the forging of business linkages between large corporations and small businesses, NMSDC continues to impact the ability of businesses to scale and reach the economic mainstream of America.

The Council's network of services and influence is as deep as it is broad. With a national office in New York and 39 regional councils across the country, NMSDC seeks to certify and match more than 15,000 minority-owned businesses (Asian-American, African-American, Hispanic, and Native American) with member corporations that want to purchase goods and services. The list of services it provides includes MBE certification, MBE referrals to corporations, membership programs for national corporate members, minority business statistics and information, educational seminars and training, technical assistance for buyers and suppliers, executive training for CEOs of minority-owned firms, business opportunity fairs, corporate and vendor directories, and networking opportunities. Through a subsidiary organization, the Business Consortium Fund (BCF), NMSDC also provides working capital loans and access to special funding.

Although Michel has not directly been a part of any alliances or joint venturing, she has nevertheless observed and facilitated numerous joint ventures during her tenure at the Council. Based upon her observations and experiences, she has concluded, like so many others have, that joint venturing and true business alliances are a phenomenon that is discussed more than it is truly exercised. Everyone says that they want to do it and are doing it. While many entrepreneurs speak of engaging in some type of joint venture, very few take the steps to make it a reality. Michel states, "Given what I have observed, I would roughly estimate that less than one-half of the alliances or joint ventures engaged in actually turn out successfully."

In the fast-paced world that many of Michel's constituents play in, it is still unusual to find successful business alliances between more than just two companies. Although the one-to-one joint venture model is the most common, three or more companies engaging in some form of alliance is not unknown. An example of this phenomenon is an ongoing joint venture between a Native American firm, a Latino firm, and an African-American firm. These companies came together to leverage a significant opportunity in the telecommunications industry.

When it comes to identifying the causes for successful joint ventures and alliances, Michel is quick to offer her insight into this matter. "Preparation is probably the one most important thing that business owners can do to position themselves to get the most out of joint venturing opportunities," she says. In cases where quick thinking entrepreneurs have successfully weathered the rocky shores of joint venturing, Michel offers the following observations as to why these firms were successful:

- In many cases, there existed a very strong impetus from a third-party player. This third-party player could be either a peer company looking to facilitate the success of another company or it could be a large corporation looking to be proactive in forming strategic alliances among its vendor base. Oftentimes, the facilitated relationship might be between a Tier 1 and Tier 2 company. This third-party participant plays the role of catalyst to make the two parties realize they are better off together than apart.

- As mentioned earlier, an incredible amount of up-front research should be conducted to assess the fit of the companies involved, to determine the "upside" of engaging in the potential venture, and agreeing on the appropriate exit strategy for the relationship.

- Successful joint venture partners engage the support of competent and experienced legal and financial advisors.

- All partners involved in a successful joint venture take the time and effort to really get a clear understanding of each other's business and develop a detailed knowledge of the terms of the deal.

- Entrepreneurs who engage in joint ventures understand that it is impossible for both companies to lead at the same time. At any given time, one partner has to be comfortable being the "senior partner" and the other the "junior partner." While this distinction might be difficult for some, co-equal management is difficult to successfully pull off, and experience has shown that it just does not work.

Tier 1 and Tier 2 Partnering Relationships

Michel has observed that success among alliances between Tier 1 and Tier 2 firms is also based upon the criteria outlined above. In these scenarios, though, often the driver of the relationship is the Tier 1 firm that is looking to identify and build a relationship with an emerging minority business. By doing so, the Tier 1 firm can help the minority business to scale in size while the Tier 1 firm penetrates promising new markets. Some of these Tier 1/Tier 2 relationships take the form of the Tier 1 partner acting as investor and the Tier 2 partner performing in a management capacity.

The majority of Tier 1 companies are major corporations that are excellent at what they do and already have the staff, physical infrastructure, and the ability to dissect, investigate, and evaluate a prospective partner. Usually these companies have already determined that there is value in going into business with a minority business enterprise before they even initiate the formalities of joint venturing. The advantage that major corporations have is that they are able to rapidly focus on firms that provide a unique market position or possess leading-edge technology.

When asked what advice she would give Tier 2 firms looking to explore joint venturing opportunities with Tier 1 firms, Michel suggests, "Small businesses should proceed with caution. They should seek the best legal and financial advice they can, so the deal is equitable and they don't end up being just a shell or front for the larger firm. Many of us in this industry are beginning to see more and more of these deals that, while legal, do not honor the intent and spirit of minority supplier development programs, and it's troubling us."

If Benefits Are So Obvious, Why Don't More Firms Do It?

Like other leaders in the small and minority business development industry, Michel is convinced that small businesses are less likely to survive in the new economy unless or until they master the art of building business alliances. The reality is that the key to growth is not just through a contract-by-contract basis but instead through an acquisition-by-acquisition basis. If a true acquisition is not in a firm's immediate plans—or within its financial reach—a "virtual acquisition" through some sort of alliance might be the next best thing.

One reason that some businesses have not made a major commitment to engaging in joint ventures is that the same entrepreneurial spirit of individualism that drove them to start the business in the first place also mitigates their desire to join forces because that would mean they would have to give up some level of control. Controlling one's own destiny is particularly a factor with some minority businesses due to the deep levels of distrust that past experiences have left ingrained in their minds. Partnerships are very difficult for strong entrepreneur types in general but are especially challenging for strong, minority entrepreneurial types because they often bring other "stuff" to the table. This "stuff" might include experiences of racism, sexism, classism, and perceived disrespect. These issues, which are often overlaid with the technical and formal arrangements of the alliance, are especially prevalent among older entrepreneurs.

In her role at NMSDC, Michel shares that she is beginning to see these extraneous issues play less and less of a role as a new generation of younger entrepreneurs are emerging in business. "Younger entrepreneurs may not have the same sort of suspicions about joint venturing because they are products of different systems in many ways," she opines. "Unlike the older generations, these young people have attended integrated schools, and if they have come from corporate America, they have already had many interactions with other communities. Thus they are more amenable to thinking outside the box and are more flexible in their approach to building their businesses."

Where Do We Go from Here?

For small businesses, in general, and minority businesses, in particular, it is critical for these firms to critique the quality of their management and their existing management structure to assure that it is in harmony with the goal of creating joint ventures. Too often, the management structure among minority businesses is very weak and limited.

According to Michel, many entrepreneurs are very competent in the services that they deliver but are less skillful at the management issues, particularly as the company grows. "When the organization is small, everyone reports to the founder," she says. "The minute you start inserting levels of management, the weaknesses of these firms become apparent. The evolution of management structure in a growing organization is a difficult transition for any company to make. Besides, small businesses have to worry about how to afford a talented management team or even knowing where to find the right people. Then, if they find the talent, they are worried people will take their business away from them. Unfortunately, many don't recognize early enough that they need a manager of some type to assume the day-to-day burden from them so they can focus on implementation of the strategic plan."

Given all the challenges that might be associated with building successful joint ventures, Michel is still convinced that America is in the midst of one of the greatest periods for minority entrepreneurs: if you have the right product, a competitive price, effective management, extensive technical knowledge and capacity, and an eye for growth through strategic business alliances, then you are poised for growth and opportunity. However, she does offer the following suggestion: "Get educated. Start online and move on from there to get trained on the process of building successful joint ventures and business alliances. Look, investigate, and learn. Learning by doing is a prescription for failure."

8

MAKING IT WORK

"Coming together is a beginning. Keeping together is progress.
Working together is success."
HENRY FORD

If strategic alliances were easy to make work, everyone would be doing them. But such relationships can go off track in ways too numerous to tally. To minimize the probability of the relationship falling into a quagmire, four areas must be addressed. These critical steps are:

1. Establishing relationship boundaries
2. Determining the initial project
3. Maintaining independence
4. Maintaining the relationship

ESTABLISHING RELATIONSHIP BOUNDARIES

Establishing and agreeing to the boundaries of a business relationship are essential for an alliance to have a chance for long-term success. Too often, companies rush into a strategic partnership without first establishing these boundaries and initiating guidelines that force the teammates to operate within these agreed-upon confines.

FIGURE 8.1 *The Fishbone System*

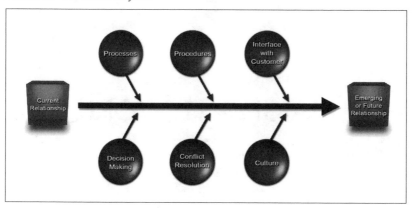

One tool I use when trying to identify and resolve the types of boundaries that need to be established when solidifying a business alliance is the "Fishbone System." This system, shown in Figure 8.1, depicts the different areas that typically "frame" a budding business relationship. Here's a description of the elements of this system.

Current relationship. The current relationship defines what the relationship looks like today in all of its aspects. This can usually be determined after the partners have had an opportunity to interact with each other a few times. Normally, the relationship interfaces will focus on three levels within the respective organizations—executive, middle managers, and knowledge-technologists.

Emerging or future relationship. The emerging or future relationship is based upon the two companies' envisioned or proposed relationship. This vision normally constitutes a best-case scenario of how the companies desire the relationship to be. Like the current relationship analysis, this analysis should also focus on the executive, middle manager, and knowledge-technologist levels.

Processes. Each company must understand the different processes that it uses to operate and manage its business and how these processes might be impacted or changed as a result of working with the other company.

Procedures. Procedures are those rules that provide guidelines and directions on how the discrete processes that make up the system are to be executed and completed. Larger companies tend to have more defined procedures than smaller companies. While small businesses often understand the need for such procedures and often will increase the number of formalized procedures as the company begins to scale, they tend to be more concerned about keeping the company operating. Thus, the focus is more on tasks that they view as critical to their short- and medium-term survival.

Interface with Customer. Interfacing with the customer is often the most contentious issue facing a new business alliance. Each partner covets this aspect of relationship building and strategically positions itself to be the face the customer sees. Two companies looking to build a long-term joint venture must first be honest with themselves and one another. It often takes years to build a working relationship with a customer. Typically, whichever partner brings the customer relationship to the alliance should be the one that leads out with the customer as long as he or she is willing to incrementally engage the partner in building a similar relationship with that customer over time. Unfortunately, large companies may struggle with this reality, especially if their partner firm is a small business. A large company's reaction is often different, though, if their partner company is another large business.

Decision making. As the companies begin to operate as a unit, everyone must be crystal clear about how decisions will be made. The hierarchy of decision-making must be established and agreed upon before any work begins.

Conflict resolution. Whenever two or more organizations are brought together to achieve a particular mission or goal, there will always be tension and conflict. That is just the way human and organizational dynamics work. The trick here is not to try to avoid conflict and tension, as so many misguided companies try to do. Instead, recognize that conflict is a part of the bonding and team-building process and must be managed like every other facet of the relationship.

The first step in managing inevitable conflicts is to define what constitutes a conflict. Every disagreement or debate among staff members is not necessarily a conflict. Companies sometimes overreact to situations in the relationship that may be contentious, unsettling, and intense, and automatically escalate them to the status of conflict. When the management team does this, it unknowingly diverts resources and attention from the critical tasks that will please the customer. The team and organization are thrown into a downward spiral.

As a rule of thumb, a conflict is an "extreme" disagreement among partners or between the company and the customer that, if left unresolved over a short period of time, will significantly put the objectives and mission of the business alliance at risk. Managing conflict is another reason why choosing a well-trained and experienced management team is fundamental to orchestrating a sustainable mode of success. Experienced on-site leadership provides the first line of defense against unwarranted escalations and can quickly and effectively deal with and deescalate any potential problems.

Agreeing to disagree is a viable option that companies often overlook. Some wrongly conclude that the outcome has to be that the viewpoint of one party must prevail. As long as the issue at hand does not put the team's ultimate success in jeopardy—and if a reasonable work-around can be developed—then it makes sense to agree to disagree and move on.

Culture. The culture of the companies that are entertaining forming a strategic alliance should never be underestimated. Culture—those values and belief systems that guide and establish the uniqueness of an organization—is one of those "soft" parameters that companies either ignore or put at the bottom of the list of factors to consider when determining the fit of a potential partner.

Without exception, a company's culture often is driven by its CEO and/or founder. This person's influence on culture is so strong and decisive that determining a company's culture is as easy as understanding what makes the CEO and leadership of the company tick. The reason why I strongly encourage prospective partners to really spend a significant amount of time together up front is to help those partners collect enough information about each other to accurately articulate each other's culture and make a true assessment on long-term fit.

Culture can make the difference between success and failure. According to T. Williams at Toyota, "In the alliances that I've seen that didn't work, the two companies were not compatible. The corporate cultures were not flexible enough to adapt. At the same time, we've had both upward and downward economic changes, and to succeed during that time, flexibility was necessary and there just was no flexibility, so these alliances died."

While the Fishbone System will guide each company through the different areas of establishing the proper relationship boundaries, it is imperative that each company engaged in the joint venture conduct the analysis on an internal company level and "drill down" into their own organization first. The results of this individual drill down is then used as input into the relationship boundaries negotiations that will ensue with the development of the new joint venture. A pictorial explanation of this process is illustrated in Figure 8.2.

DETERMINING THE INITIAL PROJECT

Determining the initial project the team will work on together is a must for all successful business alliances. Too often, companies talk about getting together and forming some type of joint venture, but the relationship never moves beyond the "talking

FIGURE 8.2 *Company-level Drill Down Analysis*

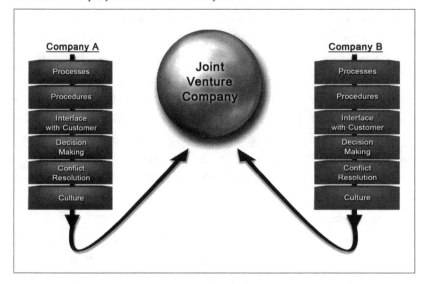

stage." As you have heard me say throughout this book, "Nothing happens until something happens."

Making something happen just for the sake of making something happen is unproductive and can, in fact, be dangerous to the individual companies and to the emerging relationship. The right project will have a high probability of success and provide real value to the team and to the customer. Guidelines for determining what the "right" project should be include the following:

- The project being considered has the commitment to success from both companies, particularly the executives of the two companies.
- The project has real value in the eyes of the customer and is not just an exercise in futility.
- The project's mission, goals, and objectives have been validated and revalidated by both companies.
- A detailed resource requirement review has been conducted, and both parties agree on the resource allocation and the timeframe in which those resources will be made available to the project.

- A detailed project timeline is established so all parties involved are clear on expectations and when the project can and should be completed.
- The project has a detailed project plan that explains *what* is to be done, *who* is to do it, *when* it should be completed, and *how* the work will be done.
- The project leadership determines what defines success for the project and who will determine when success is achieved.
- A clearly defined project kick-off date is agreed upon, and all parties are comfortable with that start date. It is better to delay the project kick-off date than to start the engagement before the team is aligned and properly focused.

MAINTAINING INDEPENDENCE

When the joint venture has run its course and is about to end, the two companies should be better off as a result of engaging in the joint venture than they were before the joint venture began. Achieving this objective is not only a function of how the deal is structured early on in the relationship, but it also depends on how much independence each company maintains during the joint venture.

How to maintain independence during the course of a joint venture is a function of what kind of deal the two companies agree to engage in. For example, if the two companies decide to both contribute resources that will be used to make up a third company, then maintaining independence might mean that both companies continue operating their original companies as they did before and pursue the operation of the joint venture company in parallel with their established firms.

I have observed many situations over the years where the two companies worked so well together that at the end of the term of the relationship, they decided to extend the term for working together, one of the companies purchased the other company, or the two companies merged. However, in situations where the alliance does not work out, each company needs to be in a position where it can continue being productive and competitive in its industry even without the help and resources from its former partner.

Of course, strategies for maintaining business independence will vary from relationship to relationship, but here are four rules of thumb that tend to work well in helping companies maintain their independence:

1. Executive management must be clear about what it needs to get out of the deal for their respective companies to remain whole. For example, if you need new technologies to automate your production process, that should be made clear. If you need new customers or deep market penetration into new territories, make that part of your business strategy.

2. Set expectations with management and staff that part of their objectives and job descriptions are to seek out new processes, procedures, technologies, and market exposure opportunities from the partner company that your company does not currently take advantage of in-house. You should be very creative in establishing lucrative incentives for your staff to pay attention to and secure these types of value-added opportunities.

3. Continue putting as much resources and creative attention into your existing business as you do with the joint venture. Attempt to grow both operations in parallel, but be careful that you don't spread yourself or your financial, operational, and creative resources too thin. Ensure continued support for current product lines and current services.

4. Institute cross-functional teams as much as possible in the joint venture so both companies are positioned to be exposed to a diverse set of functions, challenges, and opportunities. Too often, companies engaging in joint ventures

are confined to a narrowly defined band of the service delivery spectrum. While you don't want to dilute your resources too heavily, you do want to be engaged in as much of the service delivery spectrum as is possible.

MAINTAINING THE RELATIONSHIP

Once the companies in the strategic alliance have done an excellent job of establishing relationship boundaries, determining the first project, and maintaining some level of corporate independence, the final task to work on is maintaining the relationship over time. (See Figure 8.3.)

The axiom that "Rome was not built in a day" is very accurate when describing the reality of building long-term business relationships. A company might spend years and years building a productive and mutually beneficial business relationship, but it could all come unraveled by one innocent (or not so innocent) decision, misinterpretation, misunderstanding, or miscommunication. Therefore, the process of relationship maintenance should never be underestimated or ignored. If you do so, you will be putting your investment at great risk.

While relationship maintenance is a challenge with any joint venture, it often proves especially hard for smaller organizations. According to Reginald K. Layton of Johnson Controls, Inc.:

> Often, when two or more small businesses have decided to enter into a joint venture arrangement, I have observed a business dynamic emerge that tends to be different from that of large companies. With smaller companies, the egos of the entrepreneurs who started the companies tend to clash, particularly over issues surrounding management and corporate control. The process is further complicated by the fact that often small companies are used to running their businesses more informally, while forming a joint venture dictates that a higher level of business formality be instituted.

FIGURE 8.3 *Incremental Business Relationship Building*

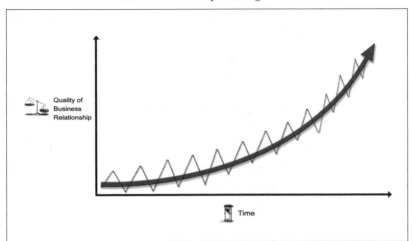

The Process of Relationship Maintenance

First, it is important to understand the "process" of relationship maintenance. As shown above, the process of maintaining business relationships reminds me of the movement and characteristics of the United States stock market. If one were to plot the value of the S&P over a long period of time (for example, 75 years), we would notice that if we looked at the change in value from a microscopic view, we would observe many small swings between appreciation and depreciation of the S&P value over that 75-year time horizon, as shown by the thin, zigzag line in the drawing above. However, if we stepped up and took a ten-thousand-foot view of the process, we would observe that although there were numerous "mini swings" in value during that timeframe, the overall trend and direction of its change in value was positive, as shown by the heavy arrow in the diagram above.

The process of relationship maintenance is very, very similar. There will be "mini-swings" in the quality of the relationship over the life of the joint venture. There will be times when the two companies are at each other's throats and prepared to march into court to resolve some issue that, on the surface, appears to be irresolvable. Conflict is a part of the relationship-building process and it does tend to temporarily "draw down" the quality of the relationship. But keep in mind that each conflict is an opportunity to expand and grow the relationship if it is properly viewed and managed.

Steps for Properly Maintaining a Business Relationship

The following steps present a proven roadmap for actively maintaining an important business relationship:

- Your perspective on the business relationship should be viewed as a marriage and not a "one night stand." A marriage view supposes that each party will commit 100 percent to the relationship's ultimate success.
- The two companies should work on nurturing respect for one another and not resentment. Companies that respect one another will ultimately work better together and produce better results and long-term value.
- Executive and middle management must be aware of what the employees' reaction is to the joint venture relationship. Being aware of this reaction requires that management listen and watch more than it speaks. Sometimes the signals of how employees are reacting will be subtle. Once management gets the first sign of discord or negativity, it should act to dispel and neutralize the point of concern.
- Identify, address, and, where possible, celebrate the cultural differences. Cultural differences between companies are not inherently a bad thing. It is the "management" of those cultural differences that determines if these differences enhance or detract from the relationship.
- Learn how to treat one another. The old biblical adage "Do unto others as you would have them do unto you" is especially applicable in managing business alliances.

- Integrate all dimensions of the relationship (e.g., strategic, tactical, operational, interpersonal, and cultural) into focusing on and achieving a positive and lasting business relationship.
- Lastly, empower and reward your relationship managers and those people responsible for the joint venture's day-to-day operation to make the critical decisions necessary for the relationship to grow and prosper. To the degree they take ownership of the success of the relationship, the quicker the two companies will be able to realize the tangible benefits a healthy relationship can bring to everyone on the team.

C a s e   S t u d y

FORGING EARLY AND LASTING ALLIANCES AT TOYOTA

In 1984, Toyota Motor Company and General Motors Corporation came together in a unique joint venture that has lasted close to 20 years. Toyota Senior Vice President Dennis Cuneo was part of the start-up team for what became known as the New United Motor Manufacturing, Inc. (NUMMI). Located in Fremont, California, NUMMI was Toyota's first production plant in the United States. With an annual production capacity of 370,000 vehicles, the facility produced vehicles for both automakers. Dennis spent 12 years with the NUMMI joint venture, which he refers to as one of the "granddaddies" of automotive joint ventures. His experience gives him a unique perspective on joint ventures, which he shares in this interview.

Of the joint ventures you've seen that have been successful, what is your opinion as to why they've worked?

Cuneo: The number-one reason is that both parties have to be committed to it and both have to benefit from it. If it is perceived that one party is receiving more benefit than the other, then I think the joint venture is doomed to failure. The second element is that the venture has to be based on mutual trust. Third, there must be a clear delineation of responsibilities in the venture. I believe it's best that one of the parties has day-to-day management control. Somebody has to be in charge, and that's a key thing.

The joint ventures that seem to work are the ones where people bring complementary skills and receive complementary benefits from the venture. One party brings the technical skills, and the other party brings the financial skills. One party may be the customer and the other the supplier. Those types of things, in my mind, tend to contribute to successful ventures.

The NUMMI venture is mutually beneficial for both GM and Toyota. Toyota runs the venture and provides the design for the vehicle; GM is the customer. GM has learned a lot about the Toyota production system from the venture. It's been mutually beneficial, and that's why it's lasted 20 years.

In terms of the NUMMI transaction, what made Toyota go with GM instead of another company?

Cuneo: Actually, Toyota first approached Ford, but they could not agree on the product to be produced. Right after that, GM approached Toyota and said, "We might be interested" and presented a proposal. The parties spent the better part of a year negotiating the agreement. In the negotiating process, they spent a lot of time getting to know each other.

What did they do to get to know each other better?

Cuneo: They visited each other's plants, studied each other's business methods, etc. The labor relations guys at GM went to Toyota plants to see what their labor relations were like and what the production system was like and vice versa. And there was a strong commitment at the top of both companies to make it work, which was critical.

Also, it sometimes helps to have a facilitator at the negotiations. We did that; we had an individual who was a facilitator and a back-channel communicator. It depends on how big the companies are; with smaller companies, it might not be as important, but it is helpful to have back-channel communications when you hit snags in negotiations. You have formal negotiations at the table where you're posturing and so on, but then you have back-channel communications to resolve critical points and float trial balloons.

In NUMMI, was there an exit plan?

Cuneo: We actually had a 12-year duration on the joint venture, mostly for antitrust reasons, but after 10 years we decided the venture was continuing to provide value, so now we have an indefinite term. I do know that some joint ventures have specific mechanisms for wrapping them up, and probably for smaller parties, it may be more important to have something like that in writing so they have some certainty at the other end.

What advice do you have for a Tier 1 firm trying to joint venture with a Tier 2 firm?

Cuneo: You have to be very clear in the delineations of responsibilities, so each partner knows exactly what it's expected to do and what the roles and responsibilities are. You also have to get a sense of the chemistry and whether these two companies can work together; sometimes you don't know that until you actually do the venture. But what I call "the mating process" is important. The venture partners should try to spend time getting to know each other.

If you're a Tier 1 firm, and seeking to do a minority joint venture, you tend to go after companies you know have been successful in your particular line of business. In automotive joint ventures, we've seen cases where a potential partner has no prior experience in the particular business at hand—and the venture didn't succeed. Taking someone who is a successful automobile dealer, for example, and trying to make them a successful supplier is not easy to do, because they're really completely different businesses.

There is a strong motivation, especially in the automotive industry, for Tier 1 firms to partner with Tier 2 minority firms, because there is such a push to increase minority content. But having said that, some Tier 1 firms wonder whether this is really a new business opportunity or just replacing an existing business opportunity. If it's the latter, there's more reluctance; they'll say, "If this is the only way I can get the business, I guess I have to do it." The most successful opportunity is when Tier 1 and Tier 2 join together, and the venture provides new opportunity for the Tier 1 to obtain a new piece of business.

What advice would you give a Tier 2 firm that wants to consider an alliance with a Tier 1 firm?

Cuneo: The more you know about the other party the better. For the Tier 2 firm, I know this is a chicken-and-egg thing, but your track record is important, especially as it relates to the industry you're getting into. A Tier I company is going to look at what your company has done, especially in this line of business or close to this line of business, that shows it can be successful.

These relationships are like marriages, and they get very messy when they break up. You may want to look at relationships that are similar to the one you're considering getting into and learn those dynamics. If you're a small firm, for example, and want to venture with a Tier I firm, the first thing is to see whether the Tier I has other joint ventures like the one you want to set up. Talk to people who are involved in that and see what makes it work. Also, a small company needs to research the bigger company to see what its corporate culture is, to see whether that small entrepreneur can function in that culture.

Any other advice that you could provide?

Cuneo: When you go into a joint venture, you have to realize that it's not easy; it's not a panacea for all things. You have to go in with your eyes open about all the problems of operating in a joint venture. Sometimes you may think, *Oh, I ought to do a joint venture with this company and it will just be wonderful and I won't have any more problems,* but what you're getting is just a different set of problems. Operating a joint venture is complicated, and you can't underestimate that.

9

LEGAL ASPECTS AND EXIT STRATEGIES

"A wise man will make more opportunities than he finds."
SIR FRANCIS BACON

After all the due diligence and self-analysis is through, your joint venture deal will finally be consummated through the completion of the legal structure and an agreement on the exiting provision. Numerous legal structures are available for use in structuring the joint venture entity.

Although the focus on the legal tasks is critical, do not allow the legal process to become so formalized and/or depersonalized that you lose the closeness and trust you have spent so much energy building prior to this step. A competent attorney/accountant team should be able to guide you to the structure that makes the most sense for your transaction. Remember, though, that these third-party professionals, while competent in what they do, do not share your vision or have the commitment to the deal that you have. Moreover, even with all of their good intentions, they do not have to live with the results of the deal, but you do. So tread carefully—measure many times, but cut once. Overall, my intent here is not to replace the advice of an attorney but to simply expose you to the options at your disposal while providing some insight into each.

MAXIMIZING THE BENEFIT FROM ACCOUNTANTS AND LAWYERS

Working with attorneys and accountants can be extremely frustrating for many entrepreneurs. I have heard many horror stories from disappointed businesspeople who have attempted to use these critical advisors only to walk away from the experience angry, disappointed, disillusioned, and with the deal left undone. Although there are no foolproof strategies for dealing with your accountant or attorney, here are guidelines for maximizing the benefit from involving these professionals in your joint venture deal. The seven rules to follow are:

1. **Be able to articulate your vision for the joint venture clearly and succinctly.** If you are unable to communicate the direction in which you want the business relationship to go, how can you expect your professional advisors to understand in what direction you are pushing the relationship?

2. **Select knowledgeable, experienced, and well-trained professionals.** The adage "a jack of all trades and a master of none" applies to many advisors. The best way to find excellent advisors is still through word-of-mouth. Find out who in the community has been putting together successful joint ventures and find out who their advisors are. Once you've narrowed your list to three good advisors, spend the time to really get to know them. There has to be good "chemistry" between your staff and theirs. When assessing their fit with your organization, don't just consider the immediate fit but the medium and long-term fit as well. You want an advisor who not only is competent but who also has the capacity to grow with your business. As your transactions become more

and more complicated, you want someone with the intellectual acumen and resource depth to support you.

3. Insist that your advisors communicate with you on your level. Too many contracts and other legal documents are written in language that a person without a legal education will not understand. Since you are paying for the information, make sure you understand it.

4. Make sure you identify any potential conflict of interests your advisor might have with your competitors. Even the appearance of a conflict should be readily addressed, even if it is with seemingly remote stakeholders involved in your transaction. If you operate in a small business community, you will probably not be able to find advisors who don't have some connection with others in your field, but you want to at least have a conversation about these links to make sure your interests will always be protected. Be particularly wary of any advisor who shares information about other clients with you. Consider whether you'd be comfortable with this person sharing similar tidbits about your business with others.

5. Be clear on who exactly you will be dealing with in your advisor's firm. Will your primary interface be with the partners or with the more junior staff? If you are unhappy with the quality or quantity of support you're getting, what will be your recourse for resolving the issue?

6. On weighty matters that may have a major impact on your deal, always be willing to seek a second opinion. Getting a second opinion does not mean you believe your counsel is incompetent or unqualified. The fact is that legal issues can often be interpreted in many different ways, and you may want or need the benefit of diverse ways of thinking.

7. Realize that the value of most attorneys and accountants usually peaks during the early part of the engagement and near the end of closing the deal. It makes sense to involve the advisors early on in the process to "frame" the opportunity, but be careful not to let them formalize and structure the deal too early. Too much structure too soon in the deal usually smothers it before it has a chance to be birthed and nurtured.

LEGAL STRUCTURES

The most prevalent options for the legal structure of a joint venture are as follows:

- Partnerships
  - General partnership
  - Limited partnership
  - Limited liability partnership (LLP)
- Corporation
  - Subchapter S corporation
  - C corporation
  - Limited liability corporation (LLC)

Below is a brief look at these legal structures. Again, as a non-attorney, my goal here is not to provide comprehensive information but rather to make you aware of the major differences in these formats. Here are the basics.

General Partnership

As stated in the Uniform Partnership Act, a general partnership is "an association of two or more persons for the carrying on of business for profit." A general partnership, however, is much more than this formal definition implies. Basically, it is a marriage between businesses consummated for the sole purpose of conducting business together to generate profits. This business relationship might be between just two companies or it could be between ten or fifty, depending on the economic mission being attempted. Regardless of the partnership's size, the rules and guidelines as to how the partners are to relate to one another and the outside world remain the same.

The advantage of a partnership is that through the partnership more resources (e.g., time, labor, capital, contacts, relationships) are made available to the enterprise so the business is able to accelerate its growth and profitability. Another major benefit to the partnership is that by having partners, the risk is spread out among a larger number of teammates, thus minimizing each individual partner's risk. This benefit is especially attractive for companies investing in new, unproven technologies or entering new markets.

The disadvantage to a partnership is that all partners have a voice in running the partnership, no matter what their individual capabilities. All profits are shared among the partners, and each partner is responsible and impacted by the business decisions made by the other partners. As mentioned earlier in this book, because of these and other risks, it's very important to spend time getting to know your potential partner because, for the partnership to function properly, you must be able to trust your partner like you would trust a brother, sister, or spouse.

There are certain authorities, rights, and privileges a partner may have in the newly formed business arrangement. These rights and privileges need to be discussed, agreed upon, and put into the agreement between the two companies. When completing the agreement, keep in mind that as long as certain acts fall within the scope of a partner's authority, all partners in the partnership have some authority to commit or bind the other partners to the consequences of their actions. A partner could typically exercise three types of authority—express authority, implied authority, and apparent authority. Express authority is a power specifically given to a partner. Implied authority encompasses the authority to commit company resources to complete tasks necessary to fulfill decisions made through a partner's express authority. For example, if a partner has express authority to conduct business development for the firm, the implied authority she has may include committing firm resources for business development tools and expenses. A partner's apparent authority enables him to do things that are legitimate and reasonable, especially within the normal practices of the partnership's industry.

Partners' rights are determined at the outset of the partnership, and the scope of such rights can vary from state to state. However, the following rights are universally included and considered in most partnership agreements:

- **Accounting on demand.** A partner has the right to review the books to determine if the information being conveyed by another partner is accurate.
- **Use of partnership property.** Whatever property is deemed to be under the partnership's ownership should be made available to all partners for use in building the business and carrying out their day-to-day functions.
- **Inspection of books and records.** There cannot be any secrets between partners. Consequently, the enterprise should be an "open book" between partners. All records and documentation should be available for review at any time.
- **Participation in management.** Each partner is a full participant in the partnership's management. Whatever governance strategy is agreed upon should be followed in the management of the organization.
- **Adding new partners.** The firm may decide to bring on a new partner. A new partner might be necessary to quickly bring a new skill onto the team. The adding of a new partner should be voted on by the existing partners, and approval should be unanimous.

- **Sharing in profits and losses.** Depending upon the percentage of ownership agreed upon between the partners, all partners have a right to share in all profits *and* absorb a portion of any losses.
- **Return of capital.** If the partnership is dissolved, and assuming there are more than enough assets left to cover liabilities, a partner has the right to be repaid his or her capital contribution to the partnership.
- **Return of advances.** Sometimes a partner makes a loan to the partnership to support the business in some way. This loan must be treated like a regular loan from a traditional lending source.
- **Indemnification.** Indemnification means to protect. It is important for partners to protect one another.

Limited Partnership

A limited partnership has both general and limited partners. The general partner assumes management responsibility and unlimited liability for the obligations of the business and must have at least a 1 percent interest in profits and losses. The limited partner has no voice in management and is legally liable only for the amount of the capital contributed plus any other debt specifically accepted.

Limited Liability Partnership (LLP)

A limited liability partnership (sometimes referred to as a registered limited liability partnership) is a general partnership recognized by its home state as a limited liability partnership. Typically, an LLP is a general partnership in all respects except for one important distinction—the partners in an LLP have no personal liability for the consequences resulting from the conduct of the other partners. All other guidelines that apply for a general partnership apply for the LLP.

Corporations

A corporation is an artificial person. It is a method of organizing a business where the business has a separate legal existence from its owner(s). This is quite different from a sole proprietorship or a partnership, neither of which can exist separately from its owners. A close corporation (also referred to as a closed corporation or a closely held corporation) is a business organized pursuant to the corporation statutes of a state, but whose stock is not publicly traded and is subject to restrictions of ownership and transfer, and where all the stockholders know each other and are actually involved in the firm's operation.

Subchapter S Corporations

A subchapter S corporation is a corporation that is given special income tax treatment by the IRS. Subchapter S of the Internal Revenue Code dealing with corporations describes this special treatment and also gives it its name. Owners of an S corporation have the same protection from unlimited liability as the owners of a C corporation, but for tax purposes, an S corporation is treated like a partnership. An S corporation does not pay taxes directly. Instead the corporation's proceeds (i.e., profits or losses) are passed down to the shareholders based on their percentage of ownership of the corporate stock. Owners are required to pay taxes on the income based upon their personal income tax rate.

C Corporations

A C corporation is any corporation that is not a subchapter S corporation. It is not necessary to do anything special to achieve this status, as any corporation is automatically (by default) incorporated as a C corporation. A corporation will continue to be a C corporation unless it applies for and receives recognition from the IRS as an S corporation. C corporations do not receive a deduction for dividends paid to shareholders. These corporations pay income tax on corporate income. Shareholders are taxed only on dividends they receive from the corporation.

Limited Liability Companies (LLC)

A limited liability company is a cross between a corporation, a general partnership, and a limited partnership. This method of organizing a business treats the company as a corporation for liability purposes, as a general partnership for income taxation purposes, and as a limited partnership for purposes of formation and, to some extent, operation of the company. In general, any business that is eligible to operate as a partnership is eligible to operate as a limited liability company.

POTENTIAL EXITING STRATEGIES

As important as deciding which legal format the joint venture should take, it is also important to determine the potential exit strategy. While it may seem odd to think about how something is going to end before it's even begun, agreeing on this up front helps avoid potentially ugly problems later on.

Thinking through the desired exit strategy forces you to carefully evaluate where you want this relationship to go. Do you see yourself partnering with this company for the long term or do you just want to achieve certain revenue objectives and then go your separate ways? These and many other questions will arise as you explore a suitable exit strategy.

You have numerous exit strategies to choose from. Some strategies are good and some not so good because they indicate a failure of the joint venture and, in the worst cases, a complete failure of the partnering companies.

Merger. The two company's boards (or the individual owners if there are no boards) agree to merge one business entity into the other. The company that is integrated into the other company ceases to exist.

End of the term. If the articles of incorporation state a specific term for the existence of the joint venture, then it ceases to exist when that designated term has expired or a specific event has occurred. Termination is typically triggered either when a specific time has elapsed or a particular event realized. The event could be based upon a single criterion or on a combination of factors such as certain profits attained, market share reached, products developed, agreement reached with customer, or a host of other possibilities. The partners should determine these outcomes up front and put them into the agreement.

Sale or purchase of assets. The assets of the joint venture are sold to another company or to individuals.

Consolidation. Consolidation is similar to merger except the end result of the transaction is different. A consolidation is when two or more existing corporations combine to form a new corporation. The original corporations cease to exist as the new corporation acquires their assets, rights, benefits, obligations, and liabilities.

Bankruptcy. This is an exit strategy you want to avoid. In this scenario, the joint venture is insolvent and files a Chapter 7 bankruptcy. Based upon this action, the corporation ceases to exist. Chapter 11 business reorganization is a different matter because a corporation can survive Chapter 11; in fact, the reason for filing for relief under Chapter 11 is to allow the corporation to find a way to survive.

Takeovers. If the stock of the joint venture company is publicly traded, the possibility exists that the corporation could be taken over by an individual, a group of individuals, another corporation, or just about any other legal entity that decides to target your corporation. Takeovers can be advantageous to the existing shareholders, especially if the investors looking to take control are willing to pay a premium for the stock.

Dissolution by shareholders. A close corporation could be dissolved at any time by any shareholder, particularly if the shareholders cannot agree on anything or are hopelessly deadlocked on a particularly critical corporate issue.

Dissolution by creditors. Creditors can petition the court for the corporation to be dissolved if it is determined that the corporation is insolvent. In some situations, creditors can even file a petition to place the corporation in an involuntary Chapter 7 bankruptcy.

Dissolution by the board of directors. The corporate entity can be dissolved by a resolution from the board of directors. However, the dissolution has to be approved by the stockholders.

C *a s e* **S** *t u d y*

SPREADING THE STRATEGIC ALLIANCE MESSAGE AT VERIZON

Verizon Communications, a Fortune 20 company with annual revenues of approximately $68 billion, is one of the world's largest wireline and wireless communications service providers and one of the largest directory publishers.

Maria D. Cruz has provided expertise to Verizon's sourcing division and currently serves as the company's executive director of supplier diversity and quality management. Here, she talks about the communications giant's views on joint ventures among its supplier base.

What has been Verizon's approach to encouraging suppliers to engage in joint ventures?

Cruz: When we dialogue with chambers of commerce or with advocacy groups representing minority or small businesses we stress that they need to educate their members about different options to help grow their businesses through joint ventures. They need to look at how companies offering similar products or services can come together to go after bigger contracts that support their growth.

Specifically, in the case of Verizon, as a large company, we're looking at national contracts or regional contracts. It's no longer local in nature for the most part. It makes sense for us as a corporation to be efficient in our sourcing process. It's more efficient for us to have ten regional contracts for IT services, for example, versus 100 contracts. That obviously has an impact on our suppliers.

If we have an opportunity for IT consultants in the Northeast and your company doesn't have enough employees to meet our requirements for such a large territory, that becomes an issue. But if you come together with a group of other small companies located in the Northeast, and, together, you have the resources we need, that increases your chance of winning our business.

Are you seeing more companies engage in alliances?

Cruz: I would say a little bit more, and I think one of the drivers has been the economy in the past few years. Some small suppliers took a major hit because they had just one major client or a couple of clients; they were not diversified enough. This has caused folks to look for partnerships, to seek out opportunities, and to try to position themselves better.

What advice would you give to companies who are interested in joint venturing to serve Verizon?

Cruz: I truly believe in growing your business and in having partnerships and alliances so you have the opportunity to bid for larger contracts. One of the most important things is to know where you fit in. I get calls from companies that say they have something to offer Verizon, and when I question them on exactly what their competencies and areas of expertise are, the answers get very vague.

For example, I got a call from a supplier that wanted to sell uniforms to us, but our workforce does not use uniforms. They hadn't done their homework. You have to do your research and really know what you do best, what we do, how we can work together, and how you can add value to Verizon. To me, that's the bottom line. The key question is: Why are you in business? You have to go back to that question first, and then you have to be able to market it effectively by telling me how you're going to solve a problem I have.

If a company had done its homework and comes to you for advice on how to identify a potential joint venture partner, what would you advise them to do?

Cruz: Often, through mainstream and trade publications we announce initiatives around new products and services, like fiber to the premises (FTTP), and identify our prime suppliers. So, a company looking to partner can easily find that information, research those prime suppliers, and then approach them with ideas on how they can help them meet Verizon's needs.

Do you encourage your prime contractors to subcontract to smaller companies?

Cruz: We have a very good subcontracting program with our prime contractors. Let me give an example in the network arena, where we need switching equipment. I don't believe there are any minority-owned original equipment manufacturers in that field. So, when we enter into these contracts with prime contractors, we have a requirement that they subcontract a certain percentage of the value of the contract to diverse suppliers.

If you can manage a relationship with one of our primes, are successful, and can offer value and meet our requirements over a period of time, that can prepare you for some possibilities to contract with us directly in the future.

Subcontracting is one of the things we suggest to smaller companies because sometimes you have to start small. You have to get into a Tier 2 relationship before you can step up to try to compete for a Tier 1 contract. It's a training ground.

What have you seen that makes the difference for contract companies to come together successfully?

Cruz: The key thing is that they have been very knowledgeable about our business. They know what we're trying to do in terms of offering products and services to our customers, so they bring value to the table. By knowing our business very well they can anticipate the direction we're headed. They know our competitive environment. They know that our customers are demanding DSL, faster service, and more products for their offices and their homes. When they know that, then they can position themselves and their products and services to add value. They can come to us and say, "We know what your environment is, we know what you're trying to do, we know what the challenges are. Here's how we can help you."

Have you seen barriers that keep companies from coming together?

Cruz: When we talk to groups about the importance of joint ventures, sometimes there is a pushback due to the fact that when you own the company and you have your name associated with it, there's a pride of ownership. That's hard to let go of. I've talked to suppliers who are reluctant to do that. Someone has to give up control, and that can be hard when you've built a business.

I think the key to success is that you come together because you find strength in each other's company and you leverage those strengths. For example, if somebody is a leader in marketing to a certain segment of your customers, then maybe that person would be the lead; if somebody has the financial background and can get funding and capital investment, then obviously that person needs to play to that strength. The control is really dynamic, depending on what you're trying to do. It's coming together, finding the strengths of the individuals and companies, and then leveraging that to move it forward.

Have you seen instances of companies building alliances that cross racial, ethnic, and gender boundaries?

Cruz: I've been aware of a couple of joint ventures that do that, and, to me, that's very good. You can talk about segmentation when you get started in business and you might get an edge with that, but eventually you really have to grow and expand. You can't say, "I'm only going to serve this particular group." Diversification is important; it's more of a multicultural society now.

To my mind, when you can cross markets and you can get a bigger slice of the pie, that's powerful. I wish I saw more of this, but I think there's more openness to looking for those opportunities now. If we've learned something in the downturn of the economy, it's to get creative and to really look at resources wherever they are. So I think the mindset is there.

Do you see any barriers to these types of alliances happening more often?

Cruz: I think there's a generational issue around this. One of the things I like about younger entrepreneurs is that they have a feeling of having no boundaries, of having limitless potential. When you have people coming out of college knowing they can be CEOs of their own companies, that's powerful.

I think older business owners might have had boundaries established for them or they couldn't get past a wall, and sometimes that has an impact on the way they do business. I believe we're going to see more joint ventures across boundaries from the younger generation.

10

WHEN LOSING IS WINNING

"Two are better off than one, because together they can work more effectively. If one of them falls down, the other can help him up. . . . Two people can resist an attack that would defeat one person alone. A rope made of three cords is hard to break."
ECCLESIASTES 4:9

Any astute businessperson will agree that today we are certainly in a great period of transition and change. Never before in human history have we seen such colossal and accelerated changes in engineering, technology, human potential, human knowledge, social structures, biotechnical developments, and world politics. Those who possess the skills and commitment to rapidly understand these changes, who can pinpoint clearly and accurately how these changes will impact their businesses, and who can develop a cohesive business strategy to respond to these changes will become masters of their own economic fate.

To do this will also require an unwavering willingness to experiment, coupled with the ability to fail without disastrous consequences. I believe the Strategic Partnership Model described in this book lays the foundation for becoming masters of our own economic fates by taking business risks and aggressively engaging in building strategic alliances—forcing us out of our comfortable approach to conducting business and thrusting us into a new realm of uncertainty *and* enormous opportunity.

However, in the case of building strategic alliances, losing really is winning. While it is true that to create effective joint ventures each participant must lose some measure of control to make the alliance work, the benefit is that the whole will be much greater than the sum of the disparate parts.

True wealth and success does not lie entirely within the solitude of our own hearts but instead resides in our ability to reach outside of ourselves, our limitations, our paradigms, our prejudices and misconceptions, and to latch on to the value, potential, and unlimited resources that other individuals, institutions, and companies can provide us. In essence, we become the perfect model for creating wealth through the sustained creation of joint ventures and business alliances.

REMEMBER THE STRATEGIC PARTNERSHIP MODEL

The Strategic Partnership Model outlined in this book works. (See Figure 10.1.) We have covered a tremendous amount of information in these pages, but as you look back on this model I want to make sure you take away the following key learnings:

Element of the Joint Venture Model	Key Learnings to Take Away from the Model
Building Trust	Nothing good happens unless you can trust one another. Spend time building trust. Trust is built through action. Commit to always following through on what you say you're going to do.
Define Mission, Goals, and Objectives	Understand why you exist and who cares that you exist.

FIGURE 10.1 *The Strategic Partnership Model*

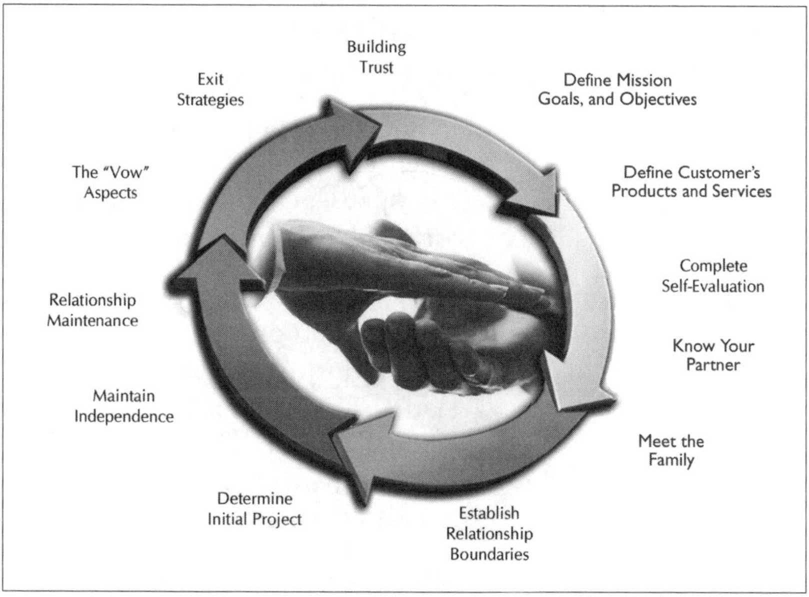

Building Trust

Exit Strategies

Define Mission Goals, and Objectives

The "Vow" Aspects

Define Customer's Products and Services

Relationship Maintenance

Complete Self-Evaluation

Know Your Partner

Maintain Independence

Meet the Family

Determine Initial Project

Establish Relationship Boundaries

Element of the Joint Venture Model	Key Learnings to Take Away from the Model
Define Customer's Products and Services	Understand what the customer needs and what resources you lack that are required to bring success to your customer.
Complete Self-Evaluation	Know yourself better than anyone else does. Understand the value proposition you bring to the team. Can the deal get done without you?
Know Your Partner	Creating joint ventures and business alliances is like getting married. Consequently, make sure you marry well. It takes time to really get to know your partner, so commit the time to make it happen early in the relationship.

Element of the Joint Venture Model	Key Learnings to Take Away from the Model
Meet the Family	Get to know your partner from a holistic standpoint. Understand all dimensions of the family (e.g., spouse, employees, vendors, stockholders, and customers).
Establish Relationship Boundaries	Like in a marriage, each partner has to understand one another so well that they instinctively know what the relationship boundaries are. There are things you should not say to your partner. There are things you should never do to your partner.
Determine Initial Project	Nothing happens until something happens. When in doubt, start small but think big.
Maintain Independence	You were successful before you met your partner; make sure you'll still be successful after your partner moves on. Complete the up-front planning and deal-structuring necessary for you to end up stronger—not weaker—as a result of the relationship.
Relationship Maintenance	Good things don't just happen. Good things have to be made to happen! Never leave the nurturing of a relationship to chance. If the relationship is worth saving, spend your time, talent, and treasure to make it better as time goes on.

Element of the Joint Venture Model	Key Learnings to Take Away from the Model
The "Vow" or Legal Aspects	Once you've outlined how you want the relationship to work, make sure you hire excellent advisors (i.e., an attorney and an accountant) to build the legal foundation and framework to support the operation of the joint venture.
Exiting Strategies	Every good thing comes to an end. Accept the fact that your business relationship will run its course and ultimately die. Don't be afraid of this reality. It is part of the cycle of business life and should be planned for just as the birth of a business relationship is planned.

Happy joint venturing! Now go out and make something happen!

C *a s e* S *t u d y*

EASTMAN KODAK COMPANY'S FOCUS ON VENTURE RELATIONSHIPS WITH START-UP COMPANIES

Through its Kodak Venture Relations group, Eastman Kodak Company has invested some $50 million in early-stage companies involved with cutting-edge technology in the infoimaging field. Kodak Venture Relations seeks investments in technologies related to Kodak's business, but more important, it acts as a liaison between start-up companies and operating units to form mutually beneficial collaborations. These relationships take various forms, including joint ventures, licensee agreements, channel partnerships, supply agreements, and equity positions in the start-up company.

As a corporate entity reporting to Kodak's chief technology officer, Kodak Venture Relations works on behalf of all operating units within Kodak—Digital and Film Imaging Systems, Graphics Communications Group, Health Imaging, Displays and Components, Global Manufacturing & Logistics, and the Research and Development organization.

Kim Pugliese is a director and vice president in Kodak Venture Relations. Here she answers questions about how her unit works with small businesses in which they have invested and/or have established commercial relationships.

Tell us how the Kodak Venture Group works.

Pugliese: As strategic investors, one of our primary criteria for investment is that the start-up strategically aligns with one of our operating units. For example, say one of our operating units has a technology it's trying to develop into specific applications, but it has a technology gap. We go into the marketplace and look for start-up companies that might potentially fill that gap. By going outside for a piece of technology or know-how, it might allow the product to get to market faster, cheaper, and more efficiently, versus trying to do all of the development work internally ourselves. Another example would be finding a start-up that could benefit by leveraging Kodak's large distribution network. Our infrastructure is already there, with its fixed costs, but if we get another product to flow through, it would lower the per-unit cost.

Sometimes, there's a real cutting-edge technology, such as in nanotechnology, and we have application areas that we're interested in, but it's very early stage. In this case, we might invest in the start-up, negotiate an observer's seat on the board, and watch how that technology develops over time.

In your career, how many joint ventures or partnerships have you either observed or participated in? How many were successful?

Pugliese: I've had a role in ten commercial relationships usually involving an equity position as well, and the success rate of the commercial deals was about 50-50.

What were the success factors for the ones that worked?

Pugliese: First, the start-up companies should find an advocate inside of a big company who will help them enter and maneuver. They have to be assured they're speaking to the right people. This is one of our roles in Kodak Venture Relations—

to assure the start-up company has the proper link to the next operating unit and the decision makers. The resources are in the operating group. So, if the start-up depends on the large company to promote their business and help them grow, they need somebody in the operating unit working with them. We use a tool called an engagement proposal, which is created with the operating unit and the start-up, that outlines an action plan with milestones, timelines, and owners.

It's also important to help each side see the other's perspective. How the start-up views the priorities and next steps can be very different from how the big company sees them, so we try to facilitate a win-win working arrangement. We make sure everyone clearly states their objectives and their expectations. We document who is going to do what, and we agree on milestones and timelines. There really are no secrets. This whole process either results in building the level of trust between the two organizations needed to increase the probability of success, or it results in the realization the relationship is not meant to be. In the latter case, it's better for everyone to look elsewhere.

Another recommendation to a start-up is to remain flexible and have contingency plans. In big companies, people change and priorities change. The start-up must realize that while they're singularly focused, in a big company, people work on many different things. So while someone may appear to be your savior, the start-up company had better be flexible, have a Plan B, and not put all its eggs in one basket. Often, there are cultural differences and priority differences; our pace and our level of bureaucracy are different than those of a start-up. But you have to sit in each other's seats to view the other's perspective and to get to a place where both parties can be successful.

We also try to facilitate constant communication. At the companies I'm responsible for, I talk to people once a week or every other week, either via e-mail or an actual conversation. We check in and make sure things are progressing as they need to.

Another factor that impacts success is that, from the big company's standpoint, we always make sure to balance our strategic objectives with the financial objectives. Our charge in Kodak Venture Relations is to help develop strategic relationships, but at the end of the day, the financial return of our portfolio matters. So at various times, what's right for us from a strategic sense may be in conflict with the long-term financial viability of the company. While we have certain milestones we want our venture allies to accomplish and certain paths we want them to go down, we realize we don't control the company. We can influence them, but we cannot force them to do anything. We need to ensure balance between our strategic objectives and the start-up's overall financial viability and need to create value. We work very hard to drive to an appropriate balance.

Here's a great example: In one deal, the Kodak operating unit wanted exclusivity from the start-up—basically to be their only customer. That may be great for Kodak and may even be great for the start-up from a short-term operational standpoint. But in the long term, a start-up company that has only one customer is most likely not going to optimize its value. Sometimes it takes significant work to help people inside the big company understand how the start-up can really help them, and why it's in their best interest to be more flexible with the negotiation and their expectations of the start-up.

It takes a lot of work.

What were the problems with the joint ventures you've seen?

Pugliese: Basically, the converse of all the things I mentioned that helped make joint ventures work. Primarily, it's false expectations and no one inside the large company helping them throughout the process, including postdeal activities.

With one of the companies I was involved in, I came in a little bit after the actual deal was done. Kodak was a channel partner, and the partner company basically thought it could sit back and Kodak would market its service. I kept telling them, "Priorities change around here so fast, so don't think that just because somebody is saying they'll do X they will, especially when there's nothing in the contract to make them do X."

In your opinion, why are many small businesses hesitant about joint ventures?

Pugliese: It's hard work. You're getting out of your comfort zone; you may have to give something up. Everybody always feels better if they can do it themselves. I think these statements are true for big companies, too. It's better to work internally; you know people, you know the processes, you know the way things are—it's comfortable and less risky, or so it seems. But in reality, by working with a start-up versus exclusively internally, one can actually mitigate risks. We constantly have to share with our people what's in it for them and why they should work with a small start-up.

Nothing is 100 percent guaranteed. There are times when it doesn't make sense for a large corporation to collaborate with a start-up, but depending on the situation, there can be advantages for both parties. Conversely, for the start-up, there's often the fear that the big company is going to come in and take control.

How can a small company that wants to do an alliance with a large company like Kodak best prepare to become more attractive?

Pugliese: Small companies need to do their homework before they start. They need to understand what it is they want out of a partnership, to be really specific: What are the objectives? If you were to have an ideal partnership, what would it look like? What would the characteristics of it be? What would you get from it? Who would do what, and on what timeline? Who are other potential partners? They need to understand why a partner is being sought, how the collaboration will work, what is being gained and what given up, and then start canvassing the marketplace for candidates.

Once they figure out who they're going after, they need to present themselves in a clear, crisp manner. Here's where some companies have trouble. While they have to be careful to protect their discovery or invention, they also need to be able to share and communicate an appropriate level of information so the potential partner can "get it." Some companies are so worried about protecting their idea that they cannot get people to understand what makes them so unique.

In addition, start-ups should know how they can benefit the big company and be able to present the vision clearly. After that, the start-up business needs to remain flexible, creative, and patient, because chances are the big company is not going to move at the pace that the start-up wants. The start-up has to be willing to accept that.

What accelerates or facilitates trust between two companies that don't know each other?

Pugliese: All of our deals include three parties: the start-up, the Kodak operating group, and Kodak Venture Relations. Certainly, the earlier the operating unit is brought into the process, the better.

Stating objectives early on also is very helpful. Honest (and frequent) communication is important in establishing a healthy level of trust. Folks doing what they say they will do, in the time period they agree to, is also helpful. It shows respect.

Sharing information is important. On both sides, people are worried about sharing too much, but an appropriate balance must be found. It's about working together to get to that win-win position.

How do you get each side to see the other side's point of view?

Pugliese: A fair amount of coaching takes place behind the scenes—more on a one-on-one basis than in a big group. But it's constantly a sales job, helping both parties understand what's in it for them. If they think there's a payoff to help them deliver on their program faster, cheaper, better—and that's what these start-ups can often do—if they can see there's a positive path forward, then the interest level goes way up. Within Kodak right now, there's a push for growth and new ideas and innovative technology. We're busier than ever, and people are more willing to consider relationships with start-ups.

What are the pitfalls of alliances with start-ups that large companies should be aware of?

Pugliese: From the large company's standpoint, doing a complete due diligence on the start-up company is a must. We had an instance where one of our operating units wanted to get a specific component, and the start-up company was going to be the sole supplier. We began an assessment of the company, since we were also interested in an equity investment, and once we began reviewing the financials, we realized the operating unit would be taking a huge risk in depending on this company for a critical component.

Another sticky area to watch is protection and ownership of intellectual property on both sides. It has to be clearly understood who owns what at the start of the relationship, and over the period of joint development.

Also, a large company has to think about the exit strategy. How is it going to get that investment to pay off? Is the start-up a company it will want to acquire over time? Is the start-up company likely to be bought by someone else, and what does that mean to strategic initiative of the larger company? These are scenarios that the investing company must consider.

SAMPLE JOINT VENTURING RELATED BUSINESS AGREEMENTS

This appendix contains a list of some of the legal documents that may be used in different types of joint venturing and business alliance arrangements, along with a few sample agreements. As was mentioned before, it is important that you consult with your attorney and accountant before engaging in any business endeavor. However, my goal for this appendix is to provide some guidelines on the types of agreements typically used for strategic partnerships, when these agreements may be used, and what they may be used for.

Agreement Title	Description of Agreement's Purpose	Where Agreement May Be Applicable
Nondisclosure Agreement (NDA)	The purpose of the NDA is to protect the confidentiality of information shared between two potential partners or two partners. Signing such agreements is a good faith gesture that indicates everyone is legally bound to keep confidential any information provided by the other party.	NDAs apply in almost all business transactions where confidential information is being shared between various companies. When in doubt, have NDAs signed by all parties.

Agreement Title	Description of Agreement's Purpose	Where Agreement May Be Applicable
Teaming Agreement	The purpose of the Teaming Agreement is to set the terms and conditions by which two or more companies plan to work together to achieve a specific objective. In most cases, the objective is to team together to win a bid. Once the bid is won, the companies usually will enter into a prime/subcontractor agreement.	The Teaming Agreement typically is applicable in loosely coupled and moderately coupled opportunities.
Joint Venture Agreement	A Joint Venture Agreement is an agreement between two or more companies (or persons) that have decided to come together to conduct a single or isolated project for a specified duration and to achieve a specified objective. Typically, the major objective is to maximize the profit from the endeavor. An example of this type agreement can be found in the *Business Owner's Legal Guide* (Knowles Publishing, Inc., PO Box 911004, Fort Worth, TX 76111; www.knowlespublishing.com).	This agreement is typically considered when the companies involved in the transaction desire to establish a more formal and tightly coupled business relationship.
Employee Sharing Agreement	The Employee Sharing Agreement sets forth the terms and conditions under which the identified employees of one company will be "shared" with the other company or by the newly formed company.	This agreement can be applicable in either a moderately or tightly coupled joint venture arrangement.

Agreement Title	Description of Agreement's Purpose	Where Agreement May Be Applicable
Stock Purchase Agreement	The Stock Purchase Agreement contains the terms and conditions under which one company will sell part of its stock to another company. In addition to the customary terms and conditions for such agreements, the agreement can also address such issues as business certifications, minority business certification, attainment of specific business goals, and other performance goals of the company whose stock is being acquired.	This agreement is mostly used in a tightly coupled joint venture arrangement where one of the partners wants to buy shares in the other company, and the acquired company becomes the legal vehicle for achieving the objectives of the joint venture arrangement.
Subscription Agreement	The Subscription Agreement is the document by which one company expresses its intent to purchase a certain percentage of the equity interest in the other company. The acquiring company gives certain representations regarding the purpose of its acquisition of the Acquired Shares and its understanding of the nature of the investment and how it fulfills criteria for exempting the Acquired Shares from the general requirement for registration of the securities with the U.S. Securities and Exchange Commission and the Secretary of State of the state in which the transaction is occurring.	The Subscription Agreement most often applies in tightly coupled joint venture arrangements in situations where one company is buying equity in another company and using the company whose stock is being acquired as the transaction engine for the joint venture.

Agreement Title	Description of Agreement's Purpose	Where Agreement May Be Applicable
Agreement among Stockholders	In an Agreement among Stockholders, stockholders agree to certain restrictions and preemptive rights in connection with the transfer and other disposition of the company stock. Principal among these is the right of first refusal of the remaining stockholders to purchase the stock of a stockholder who intends to sell such stock.	The Agreement among Stockholders may be used in a tightly coupled joint venture arrangement in which stock is transferred between the partner companies.
Employment Agreement	An Employment Agreement puts forth the terms and conditions under which a key employee will operate within the company whose stock is being purchased. Oftentimes at the end of a joint venture arrangement, one company is completely bought out and the CEO and/or management team members are invited to help transition the newly acquired company.	An Employment Agreement can be applicable for loosely coupled, moderately coupled, and tightly coupled joint venture arrangements.

EMPLOYEE SHARING AGREEMENT

THIS EMPLOYEE SHARING AGREEMENT (this "Agreement") is entered into this _____ day of _____ 2004, by and between **COMPANY A,** a __State__ corporation (the "Corporation"), and **COMPANY B,** a __State__ corporation ("Company B").

RECITALS

A. The Corporation and Company B, a __State__ limited liability company ("Company B"), are parties to that certain Stock Purchase Agreement of even date herewith, pursuant to which Company B purchased a forty-nine percent (49%) equity interest in the Corporation.

B. Company C is affiliated with Company B through one (1) or more common owners and, due to such affiliation, has an interest in the success of the Corporation.

C. Company C has agreed to provide the services of certain of its employees to the Corporation in order to facilitate the Corporation's pursuit of certain business opportunities.

NOW, THEREFORE, in consideration of these premises and for good and valuable consideration, the receipt and sufficiency of which are hereby acknowledged, the parties hereby agree as follows:

1. Loan of Employees. Company C shall provide to the Corporation the services of certain of its employees (the "Shared Employees") to fill the following positions within the Corporation: (i) Vice President and Chief Operations Officer, (ii) Director of Human Resources and Industrial Security, (iii) Vice President and Chief Administrative Officer, and (iv) Director of Business Development. The Shared Employees identified to fill the aforementioned positions and their respective salaries are set forth on Exhibit 1, attached hereto and incorporated herein by reference.

2. Cost of Employees.

2.1. Consideration. As consideration for the services of the Shared Employees, the Corporation shall pay Company C, on a monthly basis, the following:

2.1.1. For the Shared Employee in the position of Vice President and Chief Operations Officer, twenty percent (20%) of the employee's salary.

2.1.2. For the Shared Employee in the position of Director of Human Resources and Industrial Security, twenty percent (20%) of the employee's salary.

2.1.3. For the Shared Employee in the position of Vice President and Chief Administrative Officer, twenty percent (20%) of the employee's salary.

2.1.4. For the Shared Employee in the position of Director of Business Development, fifty percent (50%) of the employee's salary.

2.2. <u>Salary, Insurance and Benefits</u>. Company C shall pay directly each Shared Employee their respective salaries. Additionally, Company C shall be responsible for payment of:

2.2.1. <u>Federal Withholdings</u>. Payroll taxes relating to the Shared Employees including federal, state and local taxes will be withheld and paid by Company C. The Shared Employees shall not be treated as employees of the Corporation with respect to the services to be performed hereunder for federal or state tax purposes.

2.2.2. <u>Fringe Benefits</u>. The Shared Employees are not employees of the Corporation and are not, therefore, eligible for and shall not participate in any employer benefit provided by the Corporation including, without limitation, pension, health or other fringe benefits.

2.2.3. <u>Worker's Compensation Insurance</u>. The Corporation shall not obtain worker's compensation insurance on behalf of the Shared Employees. Company C shall comply with all worker's compensation laws applicable to its business and the Shared Employees.

3. Employment of the Shared Employees. At any time during the term of this Agreement, the Corporation may hire any or all of the Shared Employees. In the event the Corporation desires to hire a Shared Employee, the Corporation will provide Company C written notice of the same. After providing such notice, the Corporation may engage in discussions with the Shared Employee(s) the Corporation desires to hire. In the event the Shared Employee(s) agrees to be employed by the Corporation, the Corporation shall provide Company C written notice of the same (the "Engagement Notification"). The Corporation agrees that the employment starting date of any Shared Employee hired pursuant to the terms of this Section 3 will not be less than two (2) weeks from the date the Corporation provides the Engagement Notification.

4. Term. This Agreement shall have a term of one (1) year beginning the date hereof. The parties may extend the term of this Agreement upon mutual agreement.

5. Duties of the Loaned Officers. The Shared Employees shall perform those duties set forth in <u>Exhibit 2</u> attached hereto and incorporated herein by reference, as well as those duties and responsibilities set forth in the bylaws of the Corporation for their respective offices in the

Corporation, and/or those duties assigned to them by the President and/or the Board of Directors, as the case may be.

6. Trade Secrets.

6.1. <u>Confidentiality</u>. Company C agrees that the Shared Employees will keep confidential all trade secrets or confidential or proprietary information of the Corporation and its affiliates which are now known to them or which hereafter may become known to them as a result of their association with the Corporation and shall not at any time directly or indirectly disclose any such information to any person, firm or corporation, or use the same in any way other than in connection with the business of the Corporation during and at all times after the expiration of the term of this Agreement. For purposes of this Agreement, "trade secrets or confidential or proprietary information" means information unique to the Corporation which (i) has a significant business purpose, (ii) is not known or generally available from sources outside of the Corporation or its affiliates, or (iii) is not typical of industry practice.

6.2. <u>Remedies for Breach</u>. Company C acknowledges and agrees that upon a breach of this Section 6, the Corporation may remove the offending Shared Employee from his or her position within the Corporation. In the event of such a removal, the parties may, at the discretion of the Corporation, identify an individual to be provided by Company C to replace the Shared Employee so removed. Additionally, and without limiting any other remedy or right it may have, the Corporation shall be entitled to seek injunctive or other equitable relief in any court of competent jurisdiction, enjoining any such breach. The existence of this right shall not preclude any other rights and remedies at law or in equity which the Corporation may have. If any of the restrictive covenants set forth in this Section 6 are held to be unenforceable because of the duration or scope of such covenant, the parties agree that (i) such provisions shall, where applicable, be stricken, and the balance of this Agreement enforced in accordance with its terms, and/or (ii) the duration or scope of such provision shall be reduced to the extent necessary to render such provision enforceable.

7. Miscellaneous Provisions.

7.1. <u>Binding Effect</u>. This Agreement shall be binding upon and shall inure to the benefit of the parties hereto and their respective successors and permitted assigns.

7.2. <u>Headings</u>. The headings in this Agreement have been inserted solely for ease of reference and shall not be considered in the interpretation or construction of this Agreement.

7.3. <u>Counterparts</u>. This Agreement may be executed in any number of counterparts, each of which shall be an original, but such counterparts shall together constitute one and the same instrument.

7.4. <u>Governing Law</u>. This Agreement shall be construed in accordance with the laws of the State of _____ without regard to any applicable conflicts of law.

7.5. <u>Non-Assignment</u>. This Agreement shall not be assignable by any party without the prior written consent of the other.

7.6. <u>Entire Agreement</u>. This Agreement contains the entire agreement between the parties hereto with respect to the transactions contemplated herein and supersedes all other prior agreements, understandings and letters related hereto.

7.7. <u>Notices</u>. Any notice or other communications required or permitted by this Agreement shall be in writing and shall be deemed to have been duly given (i) on the date sent if delivered personally or by cable, telecopy, telegram or telex (which is confirmed), or (ii) on the date received if mailed by overnight courier or registered or certified mail (return receipt requested) to the parties at their respective places of business.

7.8. <u>Amendment</u>. This Agreement may be amended or supplemented only by an instrument in writing signed by the parties hereto. The parties hereto shall make such technical changes to this Agreement, not inconsistent with the purposes hereof, as may be required to effect or facilitate any governmental approval or acceptance of this Agreement or to effect or facilitate any filing or recording required for the consummation of any of the transactions contemplated hereby.

7.9. <u>Non-Waiver</u>. The failure of either party to exercise any of its rights under this Agreement at any time does not constitute a waiver of a breach hereof and shall not be deemed a waiver of such rights or a waiver of any subsequent breach.

7.10. <u>Severability</u>. The invalidity or unenforceability of any provision of this Agreement, whether in whole or in part, shall not in any way affect the validity and/or enforceability of any other provision of this Agreement. Any invalid or unenforceable provisions shall be deemed severable to the extent of any such invalidity or unenforceability.

IN WITNESS WHEREOF, the parties executed this Agreement as of the day and year first above written.

ATTEST/WITNESS   **COMPANY A**

_____   By: _____

                                     Name, Office

ATTEST/WITNESS   **COMPANY C, INC.**

_____   By: _____

                                     Name, Office

EXHIBIT 1

SHARED EMPLOYEES

Name	Position	Salary
Employee	(e.g., Vice President and Chief Operations Officer)	$00,000
Employee	(e.g., Director of Human Resources and Industrial Security)	$00,000
Employee	(e.g., Vice President and Chief Administrative Officer)	$00,000
Employee	(e.g., Director, Business Development)	$00,000

EXHIBIT 2

DUTIES OF SHARED EMPLOYEES

Vice President and Chief Operations Officer:

Director of Human Resources and Industrial Security:

Vice President and Chief Administrative Officer:

Director, Business Development:

STOCK PURCHASE AGREEMENT

THIS STOCK PURCHASE AGREEMENT is made as of the _____ day of _____, 2004, by and among **COMPANY A,** a __State__ corporation ("Seller"), having its principal office at [insert address], and **COMPANY B,** A __State__ limited liability company ("Buyer"), having its principal office at [insert address].

RECITALS

A. Seller is in the business of providing information technology solutions to both commercial and governmental clients.

B. Buyer and Seller desire to create a [insert type of firm] firm under the auspices of the Seller that will provide [insert description of services or product].

C. Buyer desires to acquire, and Seller desires to issue to Buyer, shares of stock of Seller representing a [insert percentage] ownership interest in Seller by Buyer, upon the terms and conditions set forth herein.

D. Buyer has executed and delivered to Seller a subscription agreement wherein Buyer proposes to purchase [insert number of shares] shares of Seller's capital stock for the Purchase Price (defined below) set forth therein.

NOW, THEREFORE, in consideration of these premises and the mutual promises of the parties hereto, each to the other, and for good and valuable consideration, the receipt of which is hereby acknowledged, the parties hereto agree as follows:

SECTION 1. Issuance and Purchase of Stock. Upon the Closing (defined below), Seller shall issue to Buyer a sufficient number of shares of the capital stock of Seller such that Buyer shall be the holder of [insert percentage] of the issued and outstanding capital stock of Seller, free and clear of all liens and encumbrances. Seller and Buyer agree that [insert number of shares] shares is the number of new shares that will be issued to Buyer hereunder (the "Acquired Shares"), and that when added to the [insert number of existing shares] shares already issued and outstanding to [insert stockholder's name] (the "Stockholder"), the total number of issued and outstanding shares of capital stock of Seller will be [insert total number of shares] shares.

SECTION 2. Purchase Price. The purchase price for the Acquired Shares is [insert purchase price] (the "Purchase Price").

SECTION 3. Payment of the Purchase Price. At Closing, Buyer shall remit to Seller the entire Purchase Price in cash, by wire transfer or by certified or cashier's check.

SECTION 4. Due Diligence.

4.1. Company Due Diligence. For a period of fifteen (15) days after the date hereof, Buyer may, through one or more agents selected by Buyer, examine Seller's books and records (the "Due Diligence Period"). Buyer and Buyer's agents will hold all of Seller's financial and competition sensitive information in strict confidence and will exercise such care to prevent the disclosure of such information to any third party as Buyer uses to protect its own financial and competition sensitive information. Buyer's obligation to purchase the Acquired Shares and to close this transaction shall be subject to its receipt of a favorable report of the Seller's financial affairs, as determined by Buyer in its sole discretion provided, however, that if Buyer receives an unfavorable report of Seller's financial affairs and decides not to close this transaction, Buyer shall give Seller written notice of Buyer's decision not later than ten (10) days after Buyer's receipt of such report. Upon Seller's receipt of Buyer's notice hereunder, this Agreement shall be deemed terminated and of no further force or effect.

4.2. Security Clearances. During the Due Diligence Period, the Stockholder shall provide Buyer with such information regarding Stockholder as is reasonably necessary for Seller to make a preliminary assessment of the Stockholder's ability to qualify for a "Top Secret" security clearance from the Defense Security Assistance Agency ("DSAA"). Buyer's obligation to purchase the Acquired Shares and to close this transaction is subject to Buyer's favorable assessment of Stockholder's ability to qualify for a Top Secret clearance, in Buyer's reasonable discretion. In the event that Buyer concludes that it is unlikely that Stockholder will qualify for a Top Secret clearance and decides not to close this transaction, Buyer shall give Seller written notice of Buyer's decision as soon as practicable but in any event not later than five (5) days prior to the Closing Date. Upon Seller's receipt of Buyer's notice hereunder, this Agreement shall be deemed terminated and of no further force or effect.

SECTION 5. Maintenance of Business Certifications. The Seller is currently certified as a Small Business and a Small Disadvantaged Business (together, an "SDB") by the U.S. Small Business Administration (the "SBA"). A listing of jurisdictions in which Seller is certified as an SDB and/or an MBE is set forth in Schedule A attached hereto and made a part hereof by reference. The parties acknowledge that in order for Seller to maintain its Small Business Development certification, the SBA must approve Buyer's purchase of the Acquired Shares. Thus, it is a condition to Buyer's obligation to purchase the Acquired Shares and to close the transactions contemplated hereunder that the SBA approve

Buyer's acquisition of the Acquired Shares. Seller will provide Buyer with copy of the SBA's decision when it is received. If the SBA does not approve Buyer's acquisition of the Acquired Shares and Buyer decides not to close this transaction, Buyer shall give Seller written notice of Buyer's decision not later than five (5) days after Buyer's receipt of the copy of the SBA's decision. Upon Seller's receipt of Buyer's notice hereunder, this Agreement shall be deemed terminated and of no further force or effect.

SECTION 6. Security Clearances: Condition Subsequent.

6.1. <u>Application for Security Clearance</u>. From and after the Closing, Seller and Stockholder shall take all reasonable steps to have Stockholder apply for and be granted a Top Secret security clearance from the DSAA. In the event that Stockholder has not received a Top Secret security clearance from the DSAA by the first anniversary of the Closing Date, Buyer shall have the right to "unwind" this transaction (the "Disengagement Option").

6.2. <u>Disengagement Option</u>. The Disengagement Option shall have a term of thirty (30) days beginning on the first anniversary date of the Closing Date (the "Option Period"), after which time the Disengagement Option will expire. To exercise the Disengagement Option, Buyer must give Seller written notice of such exercise within the Option Period. Upon Seller's receipt of such notice, the parties will agree upon a date, which will not be more than thirty (30) days from the date of such notice, upon which Seller will return the Purchase Price to the Buyer, less any portion of the Purchase Price already returned to Buyer pursuant to Section 7 of this Agreement, and Buyer will return the certificate(s) representing the Acquired Shares to the Seller, after which time neither party shall have any further obligation to the other hereunder.

SECTION 7. Performance Goals: Partial Return of Purchase Price. The Seller's right to retain the entire Purchase Price is contingent upon Seller realizing certain performance goals, as set forth in <u>Schedule B</u>, attached hereto and made a part hereof. In the event all of such performance goals are not met on or before the first anniversary of the Closing Date, then Seller will return to Buyer, upon Buyer's written demand therefore, that portion of [insert agreed-upon portion] of the Purchase Price that is commensurate with the proportion that the unmet performance goals bears to all of the performance goals set forth in <u>Schedule B</u>. Seller's demand for the return of the proportional amount of the [insert agreed-upon portion] must be made within thirty (30) days of the anniversary of the Closing Date. In the event Buyer fails to make such demand within the aforementioned thirty (30) day period, the right to make such demand shall be deemed waived.

SECTION 8. Representations and Warranties of Seller. To induce Buyer to purchase the Acquired Shares and make the investment in Seller, Seller represents and warrants to Buyer the following:

8.1. Organization and Good Standing. Seller is a corporation duly organized, validly existing, and in good standing under the laws of the _State_ and has all necessary corporate powers to own its properties and to operate its business as now owned and operated by it.

8.2. Power and Authority. Seller has the right, power and authority to enter into and perform its obligations under this Agreement.

8.3. Required Consents. Except as set forth in Section 5 or otherwise disclosed to Buyer in writing, no consent or approval of any public body or authority and no consents or waivers from any other parties to leases, licenses, franchises, permits, indentures, agreements or other instruments are required for the lawful consummation by Seller of the transactions contemplated by this Agreement. Consummation of the transactions contemplated by this Agreement will not violate any federal statute or local law, ordinance, rule or regulation or any articles of incorporation, bylaws, or resolution of Seller.

8.4. Stock Properly Issued. The Stockholder is the sole stockholder of the Seller and as such is the owner and holder of [insert number of shares] shares of the capital stock of Seller, which constitutes all of the issued and outstanding capital stock of Seller (the "Stockholder's Shares"). The Stockholder's Shares were properly issued, are fully paid and nonassessable.

8.5. Stockholders' Shares Free of Liens or Encumbrances. The Stockholder's Shares are free of any liens, encumbrances or agreements of any kind, including stockholders' agreements or voting trusts.

8.6. The Acquired Shares. When issued to Buyer, the Acquired Shares will be fully paid and nonassessable, free and clear of any liens and encumbrances, and not subject to any agreements of any kind, including stockholders' agreements or voting trusts, except for the Agreement among Stockholders between the parties hereto that is contemplated by this Agreement at Section 10.

8.7. Corporation's Assets. Schedule C attached to this Agreement and made a part hereof, lists and describes each asset owned by Seller as of the date of this Agreement including, without limitation, all real property owned by or leased to the Seller. Unless otherwise stated, Seller is the sole owner of each asset. None of the assets is subject to any liens or encumbrances except as otherwise stated in Schedule C.

8.8. <u>Corporation's Liabilities</u>. <u>Schedule D</u> attached to this Agreement and made a part hereof, lists and describes Seller's debts and liabilities as of the date of this Agreement, including the name and address of each of Seller's creditors, the amount owed to each creditor, and the last date on which the debt or liability may be paid or discharged.

8.9. <u>Corporation's Financial Condition</u>. <u>Schedule E</u> attached to this Agreement and made a part hereof, is a true and accurate copy of the most recent financial statements of Seller, consisting of a balance sheet as of [insert date] and an income statement for the year ended [insert date]. The attached financial statements present a true and accurate description of the financial condition of Seller as of the dates indicated. There will be no material changes in Seller's financial condition as set out in the balance sheet between the date of the balance sheet and the closing of this transaction except for those changes that will normally occur in the regular course of Seller's business.

8.10. <u>No Suits Pending or Imminent</u>. There are no actions at law or equity or administrative proceedings pending against Seller or in which Seller is a plaintiff, defendant, petitioner or respondent, except as listed on <u>Schedule F</u> attached hereto and made a part hereof. Seller does not propose to commence an action at law or equity or an administrative proceeding in which it will be a plaintiff or petitioner. There are no actions at law or equity or administrative proceedings pending in which it is anticipated that Seller will join or be joined as a party.

8.11. <u>No New Contracts Before Closing</u>. Seller will not enter into any new contracts or agreements between the date of this Agreement and the Closing except in the ordinary course of business.

8.12. <u>No Dividends</u>. The Board of Directors of Seller have not declared any dividends since the date of the balance sheet attached to this Agreement and more fully described in Section 8.9. There are no dividends unpaid that were declared in an earlier period. From the date of this Agreement to the Closing, the Board of Directors of Seller will declare no dividends.

8.13. <u>No Salary Increases; No New Employees</u>. From the date of this Agreement to the Closing, Seller will not increase any employee's salary or hire any New employee without first obtaining Buyer's written consent.

8.14. <u>Going Business</u>. At the time of the Closing, Seller will be a going business. If this warranty is breached, Buyer may terminate this Agreement and demand the return of any sums Buyer has paid Seller on account of the Purchase Price of the Acquired Shares. Upon Seller's return of those sums and Buyer's return of the stock certificate(s) representing the Acquired Shares, this Agreement shall terminate and be of no further force or effect, and Buyer and Seller shall have no further rights against or obligations to each other.

8.16. <u>Officers and Directors</u>. The officers and directors of Seller are set forth on <u>Schedule G</u> attached hereto and made a part hereof. From the date of this Agreement to the Closing, Seller will not elect any other or additional directors or appoint any other or additional officers.

8.17. <u>Existing Employment Contracts</u>. <u>Schedule H</u> contains a list of all of Seller's material employment contracts and pension, bonus, profit-sharing, stock option or other agreements providing for employee re-muneration or benefits. To the best of Seller's knowledge, Seller is not in default under any of these Agreements.

SECTION 9. Buyer's Representations and Warranties. To induce Seller to sell the Acquired Shares, Buyer represents and warrants to Seller the following;

9.1. <u>Organization and Good Standing</u>. Buyer is a limited liability company duly organized, validly existing, and in good standing under the laws of the ____State____ and has all necessary corporate powers to own its properties and to operate its business as now owned and operated by it.

9.2. <u>Power and Authority</u>. Buyer has the right, power and authority to enter into and perform its obligations under this Agreement.

9.3. <u>Required Consents</u>. No consent or approval of any public body or authority and no consents or waivers from any other parties to leases, licenses, franchises, permits, indentures, agreements or other instruments are required for the lawful consummation by Buyer of the transactions contemplated by this Agreement. Consummation of the transactions con-templated by this Agreement will not violate any federal statute or local law, ordinance, rule or regulation or any articles of organization, operat-ing agreement or resolution of Buyer.

SECTION 10. Agreement among Stockholders. At the Closing and as a condition thereof, Seller and Buyer will execute and deliver, one to the other, an Agreement among Stockholders, the form of which is at-tached hereto as <u>Exhibit 1</u>, and is incorporated herein by reference.

SECTION 11. Employee Sharing Agreement. Buyer is affiliated with and/or has a relationship with Company C ("Company C"). At the Clos-ing, and as a condition thereof, Buyer shall cause Company C to enter into an Employee Sharing Agreement with the Seller, the form of which is attached hereto as <u>Exhibit 2</u>, and is incorporated herein by reference.

SECTION 12. Employment Agreement. At the Closing, and as a condition thereof, Seller and Stockholder will enter into an employment agreement, the form of which is attached hereto as Exhibit 3, and is incorporated herein by reference.

SECTION 13. Documents to Be Delivered to Buyer at Closing. At the Closing, Seller shall deliver to Buyer the following:

13.1. Stock Certificates. A stock certificate representing [insert number of shares] shares of Seller's capital stock, fully paid and nonassessable;

13.2. Opinion of Seller's Counsel. An opinion of Seller's counsel regarding such matters as litigation, Seller's power and authority to enter into this Agreement and consummate this transaction, Seller's compliance with laws and such other matters relevant to this transaction;

13.3. Stockholders' Agreement. The Agreement among Stockholders, the form of which is attached hereto as Exhibit 1, that is to be entered into by the parties hereto, among others, at the Closing; and

13.4. Employee Sharing Agreement. Copy of the Employee Sharing Agreement, the form of which is attached hereto as Exhibit 2 that is to be entered into by the parties thereto at the Closing.

SECTION 14. Documents to Be Delivered to Seller at Closing. At the Closing, Buyer shall deliver or cause to be delivered to Seller the following:

14.1. Purchase Price. A certified or cashier's check in the amount of the Purchase Price made payable to Seller;

14.2. Opinion of Buyer's Counsel. An opinion of Buyer's counsel regarding such matters as litigation, Buyer's power and authority to enter into this Agreement and consummate this transaction, Buyer's compliance with laws and such other matters relevant to this transaction;

14.3. Stockholders' Agreement. The Agreement among Stockholders, the form of which is attached hereto as Exhibit 1, that is to be entered into by the parties hereto, among others, at the Closing;

14.4. Employee Sharing Agreement. The Employee Sharing Agreement, the form of which is attached hereto as Exhibit 2, that is to be entered into by the parties thereto at the Closing; and

14.5. Employment Agreement. The Employment Agreement, the form of which is attached hereto as Exhibit 3, that is to be entered into by the Stockholder and the Seller at the Closing.

SECTION 15. Election of Officers. Seller agrees that immediately after the Closing, Seller's board of directors will elect the following persons to the respective offices following their names:

Name   President and Chief Executive Officer

Name   Vice President and Chief Operations Officer

Name   Director of Human Resources

Name   Vice President and Chief Administrative Officer

Name   Director, Business Development

Seller agrees to amend its bylaws to contemplate these above-described offices within the corporation if necessary. The offices described herein shall have the duties and responsibilities set forth in <u>Exhibit 4</u>, which is attached hereto and incorporated herein by reference.

SECTION 16. Time and Place of Closing. The closing (the "Closing") shall take place at the offices of Seller, located at [insert address], on or before _____, 2004 (the "Closing Date"), or such other time and/or place as the parties may agree upon in writing.

SECTION 17. Expenses of Transaction. The parties shall share equally the costs and expenses of this transaction including, without limitation, the professional fees incurred by either party.

SECTION 18. Agreement Binding. This Agreement is binding upon and shall inure to the benefit of the parties' heirs, executors, administrators, representatives, successors and assigns.

SECTION 19. Applicable Law. This Agreement shall be constructed in accordance with the laws of ___State___, the state in which Seller is incorporated.

IN WITNESS WHEREOF, each of Seller and Buyer has caused its name to be hereunto subscribed by its duly authorized officer, all as of the day and year first written above.

WITNESS/ATTEST: **COMPANY NAME A (SELLER)**

_____   By: _____
                                      NAME, President

WITNESS/ATTEST: **COMPANY NAME B (BUYER)**

_____   By: _____
                                      NAME, Managing Member

Stockholder hereby executes this Agreement solely for the purpose of acknowledging his obligations as set forth in Sections 4.2 and 12 of the Agreement.

WITNESS:

_____   By: _____
                                 Stockholder, individually

SUBSCRIPTION AGREEMENT

Company A
Street Address
City, State Zip Code

Ladies and Gentlemen:

The Company B, a ___State___ limited liability company ("Company B"), proposes to purchase from Company A, a ___State___ corporation, (the "Company"), [insert number of shares] shares of its common stock (such shares being hereinafter referred to as the "Shares") for an aggregate purchase price of [insert price].

Company B understands that the Shares are not registered with the Securities and Exchange Commission (the "SEC") under the Securities Act of 1933, as amended (the "Act"), and are to be sold and issued pursuant to the exemption, among others, provided by Section 3(b) of the Act relating to certain small, non-public offerings. Company B also understands that the Shares have not been qualified in ___State___ or under the securities laws of any other state and are to be sold and issued pursuant to the exemption from qualification in ___State___ provided by Section 00-000(0) of the ___State___ Securities Act.

To induce the Company to sell and issue the Shares, and understanding that the Company will rely thereon in foregoing registration of the Shares under the Act, Company B warrants and represents as follows:

1. Company B is acquiring the Shares for investment, for its own account and not with a view to or for sale in connection with any distribution thereof or with any intention of disposing of the same or any interest therein.

2. Company B's purchase of the Shares has not been accompanied by the publication of any advertisement, or any form of general solicitation.

3. Company B understands that the Shares must be held indefinitely unless subsequently registered under the Act and qualified under applicable state securities laws or unless an exemption from such registration and qualification is applicable to any subsequent transfer. Company B hereby agrees that the Shares will not be sold without registration under the Act and qualification under applicable state securities laws or exemption therefrom. Company B understands that the Company has no present plans for registration or for qualification of the Shares and that the Company has no obligation to register or to qualify the Shares for any future sale thereof by Company B.

4. Company B is aware of the terms of Rule 144 adopted by the SEC under the Act, relating to the conditions under which "restricted securities" (which term may include the Shares) may be transferred without registration under the Act. Company B understands that Rule 144 may not be available for future transfers of the Shares occurring even after the expiration of two years after the full purchase price for the Shares has been paid because information meeting the requirements of Rule 144(c) may not be publicly disseminated by the Company. Company B further understands that the Company has no obligation to Company B ever to disseminate information so as to make Rule 144 available for future transfers of the Shares.

5. Company B understands that the Shares are subject to the restrictions on transfer in the legends to be imprinted on the certificates evidencing the Shares which legend shall read substantially as follows:

THE SECURITIES REPRESENTED BY THIS CERTIFICATE HAVE NOT BEEN REGISTERED UNDER THE SECURITIES ACT OF 1933, AS AMENDED, UNDER THE ___State___ SECURITIES ACT, OR UNDER THE SECURITIES ACTS OF ANY OTHER STATE OR JURISDICTION. NO SALE, OFFER TO SELL OR OTHER TRANSFER OF THESE SECURITIES MAY BE MADE UNLESS PURSUANT TO AN EFFECTIVE REGISTRATION STATEMENT, OR UNLESS IN THE OPINION OF COUNSEL OF THE ISSUER, THE PROPOSED DISPOSITION MAY BE MADE PURSUANT TO A VALID EXEMPTION FROM THE REGISTRATION PROVISIONS OF THOSE ACTS.

6. Company B has had access to financial information about the Company and all such other information concerning the Company as Company B has requested and Company B has had the opportunity to discuss the investment with and ask questions of officers or other appropriate representatives of the Company; Company B has such knowledge and experience in financial and business matters that it is capable of evaluating the risks inherent in the proposed purchase of the Shares; Company B has assets and income that it is able to bear the risk of the

loss of the entire investment; Company B has evaluated all information about the Company it deems material to the formulation of an investment decision, and does not desire any further information or data concerning the Company.

7. Company B agrees that the Company may note upon its stock transfer records a "stop transfer order" with respect to the Shares in order to enforce the restrictions on transfer hereinabove described. Company B understands and agrees that any and all share certificates issued by the Company to Company B in connection with the proposed purchase may bear the restrictive legends hereinabove described. Company B further agrees that the Company shall not be liable for any refusal to transfer the Shares upon the books of the Company, except in compliance with the terms and conditions of such restrictions.

8. Company B agrees to indemnify, save and hold harmless the Company, its successors and assigns, and their officers, directors and controlling person, if any, against any loss, claim, damage, liability, cost and expense rising out of breach by Company B of any of the foregoing representations, warranties and covenants, whether under the Act, as the same may be amended from time to time, the securities laws of any state, or otherwise. Finally, Company B agrees that the terms and conditions of this letter shall also bind its successors and assigns.

WITNESS: **COMPANY B**

_____   By: _____
                                                    Name, Office

I n d e x

A

Accountants, 156–58, 175
Accounting on demand, 160
Acquisitions, 3, 135–36
  company cultures and, 3
  Procter & Gamble and, 44
Advisors, 134, 156–58, 175
African-Americans, xii, 69, 71
Aging population, 2
Alliances. *See* Strategic alliances
Allston, Tim, 35–40
Allston Communications Inc., 35
Amos Tuck School of Business
  Administration, 1, 61
AOL, 4
Apartheid, 34
Apparent authority, 160
Apple, 4
*Are Our Egos Destroying Us?
  Confessions of a Recovering
  Ego-holic* (Allston), 36
Articles of incorporation, 164
Art of War, The (Sun Tzu), 23
Asian-Americans, xii, 69, 71
Assets, sale or purchase of, 164
AT&T, 3, 75
Attitude adjustment, 68–69
Attorneys, 156–58, 175
Authority, 105, 159–60
Axion, 88–89

B

Back-channel communications, 151
Bacon, Sir Francis, 155
Bankruptcy, 164
Benefits, mutual, 83–85

Biases, 72–73
Blood and Guts Entrepreneurs,
  99–100
Blue Skyers, 130
Board of directors, dissolution by,
  165
Boulder analogy, 92–93
Brandenburger, Adam, 4
Broadview Group/Broadview
  Staffing Services, 92–97
Brown Bombers Entrepreneurs, 101
Bundling of contracts, 31
Business Consortium Fund, 133
But Syndrome, 28–29

C

Capital, organic growth and, 2
Carlyle Group, 88
C corporations, 162–63
CEOs, 7, 143
Chapter 11 business reorganization,
  164
Chapter 7 bankruptcy, 164, 165
CHESS factor, 29–34
  competition, 29–32
  economic climate, 32–34
  historic influences, 32
  societal events, 34
  strategic alliances, 34
Civic affairs, 26
Close (closed) corporation, 162
Commitment, 93, 150
Communication
  attitude/process/procedure
    adjustment and, 68–69
  attorneys/lawyers and, 157

Communication (continued)
  back-channel communications,
    151
  feedback solicitation, 68
  key personnel and, 107
  trust and, 65
Communism, 34
Community involvement, 26, 114–16
Compass Group USA, 76–77
Competition, 29–32
  analysis of, 108–11
  size of, 109
Conflict resolution, 56, 141–42
Conflicts of interest, 157
Consolidation, 164
Consultants, retired workers as, 58
Consumers, 89
Contingency plans, 177
Contract bundling, 31
Contractor/subcontractor
  relationships, 13
Co-opetition, 3–4
Co-opetition (Brandenburger and
  Nalebuff), 4
Core competencies, 12, 60
Corporations, 162
  company culture, 3, 142–43
  personality groups of, 129–31
Creditors, dissolution by, 165
Credit reports, 126–27
Cruz, Maria D., 165–69
Cultural differences/
  misunderstandings, 6, 49, 149
Culture (company), 3, 142–43
Cuneo, Dennis, 150–53
Customer(s)
  customer interface, 141
  defining products/services for,
    173
  relationship building, 105
  target, 50–51, 85
Customer economy, xi
  cultural misunderstanding and,
    6
  organic growth and, 2

D

Daring Dashing Dans and Dianes,
  102
D&B credit reports, 126–27
Decision making, 141
Dell, 76–77
Demographics
  aging population, 1–2
  ethnics and economic clout, xii
Deregulation, 4
Detail, attention to, 73–74
Discrimination, perceptions of,
  71–72
Dissolution by creditors/share-
  holders/board of directors, 165
Distribution strategy, 106–7
Dollar volume, 109
Doomers, 129
Downsizing, xii–xiii, 33–34
Drill Down Analysis, *144*
Drucker, Peter F., 1
Due diligence, 51, 119–37, 180
  assessing LLIFT, 121–28
  categorizing potential partner,
    128–31
  tendency to avoid, 120–21

E

Eastman Kodak Company, 175–80
Economic climate, 32–33
  goals and, 89
  world, 2
Ehrlich, Robert L., 18
80/20 principle, 40
Empire Builders, 102
Employee reactions to joint venture,
  149
Employee Sharing Agreement,
  185–89
End of the term, 164
Engagement proposal, 177
Entrepreneurial preparedness. *See*
  Preparedness categories
Ethnic diversity, xii, 69–73
Exit strategies, 15, 54, 152, 163–65,
  175, 180
Express authority, 159–60

F

Facilitators, 151
Failure, 7
Feedback solicitation, 68
Fence Walkers, 101–2
First-step project, 52–53
Fishbone System, 140–43, *140*
Flexibility, 177
Ford, Henry, 139
Ford Land Development
    Corporation, 59
Ford Motor Company
    Minority Supplier Development
        Program, 30–31
    supplier alliances and, 56–60
Forgiveness, 75
Freddie Mac, 114–18
Free Agent Nation (Pink), 40

G

General Motors Corporation, 150–51
General partnership, 158–61
Globalization, 2, 33
    impact of, 109–10
    Procter & Gamble and, 43
Goals, 89–91, 172
    controllable/uncontrollable
        factors, 89–90
    defining, 49–50, 172
Going deep, 12
Government regulations, 89, 111
Growth
    joint venturing and, 23–34
    risk and, 107
    strategies, 2–4
Gut instincts, 63–64

H

Hammerstein, Oscar, 119
High Impact Marketing, 35
Hispanic Americans, xii, 69, 71
Historic influences, 32
Honesty, 64, 74
Housing, 114–18
Humphreys, Jeffrey M., xii

I

IBM, 4
Immigration, 2
Implied authority, 160
Indemnification, 161
Independence, 53, 145–47, 174
Industry analysis, 108–11
Infinity Technology, 35
Infrastructure, 12
Initial project, determining, 143–45
Inouye, Jay, 114, 116–18
Integrity, 37–38
Intellectual property, ownership
    of, 180
Internet, 19, 33
Intuition, 131–32

J

Jenkins, Gwen, 92–97
Jensen, Ray, 56–60
Jo-Harry Window group process
    model, 66
Johnson Controls, Inc., 48, 147
Joint venture/joint venturing, 3–4,
    5–15
    see also Strategic alliances
    business agreements, 181–200
    business growth and, 3
    continuum, 9–15, *10*, 126
    defined, 7–9
    economic factors, xi–xiii
    growth and. *See* Growth
    incentives for, 23–25, *24*
    legal issues, 13
    loosely coupled, 10–11, 14, 15
    mission of, 8–9, 49–50, 172
    moderately coupled, 11–13,
        14, 15
    obstacles, 5–6
    preparedness, 99–103, *100*, 134
    State of Maryland Office of
        Minority Affairs and, 16–21
    success of, 134–35, 150–51,
        177–78
    supporting elements, 9
    tightly coupled, 13–14
    timing and, 6–7
Juzang, Guy, 35

K

Keller, Helen, 47
Know Yourself Model, 65–69, *66*
Kodak Venture Relations Group,
 175–80

L

Latino-Americans, xii, 69, 71
Lawyers, 156–58, 175
Layton, Reginald K., 48, 147
Legal issues, 13, 54, 155–58, 175
 see also Exit strategies; Legal
  structures
 accountants and lawyers, 156–58
Legal structures, 158–63
 C corporations, 162–63
 corporations, 162
 general partnership, 158–61
 limited liability companies, 163
 limited liability partnership, 161
 limited partnership, 161
 subchapter S corporations, 162
LIFO approach, 100
Limited liability companies, 163
Limited liability partnership, 161
Limited partnership, 161
LLIFT model, 122–28
 financial muscle/commitment,
  126–28
 interest/incentive, 125–26
 likeability, 122–24
 longevity, 124–25
 timeline, 128
Lombardi, Vince, 99

M

Management
 employees' reactions to joint
  ventures and, 149
 empowerment, 150
 issues, 136–37
 middle management, downsizing
  and, xiii
Marketing strategy, 108
Market(s)
 market access, 25, 27

 new and emerging, 3
 share, 110
 size, 109
Maryland's Minority Business
 Enterprise Program, 16–21
Mentor/protégé relationship, 97
Mergers, 14–15, 146, 164
Michel, Harriet, 133–37
Microsoft Corporation, 4, 75–79
Millennium Group, 88
Minorities
 breaking down perceptions,
  69–73
 businesses of. *See* Minority-
  owned businesses
 cultural misunderstanding and,
  6, 49
 economic clout of, xii
 harmony among, 72
 interracial/interethnic contact,
  71
Minority-owned businesses, 38–39
 automotive industry and, 152
 federal government and, 31
 Ford's Minority Supplier
  Development Program, 30–31
 Freddie Mac and, 116–18
 market access and, 25, 27
 Maryland's Minority Business
  Enterprise Program, 16–24
 National Minority Supplier
  Development Council and,
  133–37
 perceptions and, 70
 Procter & Gamble supplier
  diversity program and, 41–46
 technology and, 57–58
 Toyota's Opportunity Exchange
  and, 30
Mission/mission statement, 8–9,
 49–50, 86–89, 172
 analysis of, 104–5
 of potential partner, 125
MOGO, 81–97
 case study, 92–97
 development guidelines, 82–86
 goals and objectives, 89–91
 mission statement, 86–89

opportunity, 91–92
relevance to, 105
Money, 86
Motivation, 87

N

Nalebuff, Barry, 4
National Conference for Community
& Justice, 70–71
National Minority Supplier
Development Council Inc., 133–37
Native Americans, xii, 69
Natural Entrepreneurial Economy,
xii–xiii
Need fulfillment, 39–40
Networking, 26, 40
Newton, Isaac, 65
New United Motor Manufacturing,
Inc., 150–52
Niche marketing, 32
Nickerson, Craig, 114–16

O

Objectives, 49–50, 89–91, 172
Opportunity
defining, 91–92
identifying, 112

P

Partners/partnership(s)
categorizing potential, 128–31
due diligence and, 119–37, 173
finding, 26–27
general, 158–61
limited, 161
limited liability, 161
partners' rights, 160–61
selection criteria, 96–97
Personality groups, 129–31
Personnel, identifying key, 107
Pinder, Sharon R., 16–21
Pink, Daniel, 40
Population
aging and decline of, 2
diversity of, 69
shifts, xii

trend analysis, 110
Power base, building, 105
Preparedness categories
Blood and Guts, 99–100
Brown Bombers, 101
Daring Dashing Dans and
Dianes, 102
Fence Walkers, 101–2
Pricing strategy, 106
Prime contractor/subcontractor
relationships, 13
Procedure(s)
adjustment, 68–69
defining, 141
Process(es), 140–41
adjustment, 68–69
engagement, 64
Procter & Gamble, 41–46
Product(s)
defining, 50, 173
types, listing, 106
Production site capabilities, 107–8
Productivity, xiii
Progress reports, 74
Project
determining initial, 143–45
start date, 145
Pugliese, Kim, 176

R

Race relations, 72
Real estate, 8
Registered limited liability
partnership, 161
Regulatory influences, 89, 111
Relationship
boundaries, 52, 139–43, 174
building, 48, 62. *See also* Trust
maintaining, 53, 147–50, 174
process of, 148–49
steps, 149–50
Reliability, 74
Reluctant Warriors, 129–30
Resource requirements, 144
Respect, mutual, 74
Revenue stage, 77
"Right-sizing," 2

Risk(s), 65
    analysis of, 127
    growth and, 107
    partnerships and, 159
Robinson, Dan, 33, 62

S

Sale, of assets, 164
Sales, Michael Sr., 35–40
Sanders, Jerry, 92–97
Self-employment, 34
Self-evaluation, 51, 173
    analysis, 104–8
    preparedness categories, 99–103
    SWOT exercise, 111–13, 127
Selig Center for Economic Growth,
    xii
September 11 attacks, 1
Services, defining, 50, 173
Shadowing, 58
Shakespeare, William, 51
Shareholders, dissolution by, 165
Small Business Administration, 122
Smith, G. Winston, 75–79
Smorgasbord Joint Ventures, 35, 37
Societal events, 34
Start date, 145
Start-up companies, Kodak and,
    175–80
Steele, Michael S., 18
Stock Purchase Agreement, 190–98
Strategic alliances, xiv–xv, 3–4
    see also Joint venture/joint
        venturing
    Fishbone System, 140–43, 140
    initial project, determining,
        143–45
    maintaining independence,
        145–47
    maintaining the relationship,
        147–50
    relationship boundaries, 139–43
    small company challenges,
        94–95
Strategic Partnership Model, 47–60,
    49, 172–75, 173

building trust, 49, 60, 62–63.
    See also Trust
complete self-evaluation, 51
conflict resolution, 56
customers/products/services
    defined, 50
exit strategies, 15, 54
first-step project, determining,
    52–53
Ford Motor Company and,
    56–60
goal of, 54–56
knowledge of partner, 51
legal aspects, 54
maintaining independence, 53
meet the "parents," 51–52
mission, goals, objectives
    defined, 49–50, 172
relationship boundaries, 52, 174
relationship building, 48
relationship maintenance, 53,
    174
Strengths, identifying, 111, 112–13
Subchapter S corporations, 162
Subscription Agreement, 198–200
1Sun Tzu, 23
Supplier(s), 85, 89
    agreement on, 85
    diversity
        Ford Motor Company and,
            30–31
        Freddie Mac and, 114–18
        Microsoft Corporation and,
            75–79
        Procter & Gamble, 41–46
        Verizon Communications and,
            167, 168
Support services, 86
SWOT exercise, 111–13

T

Takeovers, 165
Taking America's Pulse, 70–72
Target customers, 50, 85
Teams, cross-functional, 146–47
Technology, 89
    acquisitions and, 3
    analysis of emerging, 110

co-opetition and, 4
global economy and, 2
neutralization of time/space
    by, xi
sharing, 11
supplier relationships and,
    57–58, 59
Thompson Hospitality, 76–77
Threats, identifying, 112
Tier 1 and 2 strategies, 78, 135,
    152–53
Timeline, 128, 145
Timing, 6–7
Toyota Motor Company, 143, 150–53
    "Opportunity Exchange," 30
Trade missions, 18
Trends, analysis of, 110
TriTech, 59
Trust, 49, 60, 61–79, 82, 96, 150, 172
    attention to detail, 73
    attitude, process, and procedure
        adjustment, 68–69
    building, 62–63
    commitment to forgive, 75
    communication and, 64
    determining leader/follower, 75
    honesty, 74
    Know Yourself Model, 65–69
    mutual respect and, 74
    perceptions, breaking down,
        69–73
    process engagement, 64
    reliability, 74
    responding honestly, 67–68
        trust-building model, 63, 63–65
        values and gut assessment,
            63–64
Tuck, Edward, 61

U–V

Uniform Partnership Act, 158
Values, 63–64, 87
Vendors. See Supplier(s)
Verizon Communications, 165–69
Virginia Minority Supplier
    Development Council, 117
Virtual partnerships, 11
Vision, 87, 104–5

W–X

Weaknesses
    exposing, 12
    identifying, 112–13
Williams, Icy, 41–46
Williams, T., 4, 30, 131, 143
Women-owned businesses, 16, 18–21
    federal government and, 31
    Ford strategic model and, 60
    Freddie Mac and, 117–18
    market access, 25, 27
    Procter & Gamble supplier
        diversity program and, 41–46
World economy, 2
Worldwide Technology, 76–77
Xerox Corporation, 33, 62